BECOMING
COMMUNITY

BECOMING COMMUNITY

Meeting in the Intersection of Truth and Love

OLIVIA A. PHILLIPS

WIPF & STOCK · Eugene, Oregon

BECOMING COMMUNITY
Meeting in the Intersection of Truth and Love

Wipf & Stock
An Imprint of Wipf and Stock Publishers
199 W. 8th Ave., Suite 3
Eugene, OR 97401

www.wipfandstock.com

PAPERBACK ISBN: 978-1-6667-1637-5
HARDCOVER ISBN: 978-1-6667-1638-2
EBOOK ISBN: 978-1-6667-1639-9

10/12/21

I write for you.

Contents

Part Three | Ministries That Make a Difference

Preface

I write this book for the many individuals that have been hurt by the moments when we have gotten things wrong. I write for those who have suffered when we have used Scripture as a weapon instead of as the source of our great hope and love.

For the family who, in the Fall of 2008, were forced to move out of the area by their relentless acts of violence and hatred committed by the local Christian community towards their *teenage* daughter who identified as lesbian.

For the child who, in 2009, was told by their Christian mother that they were no longer welcomed in their home because they decided to embrace a gender identity that did not match their birth sex.

For the young woman who, on Christmas Eve 2011, was outed by her mentor and pastor—for the sake of protecting others from her queerness, and now suffers from ongoing struggles with depression.

For the parent who worried that their child would face hate because they were struggling to understand their identity within a binary system of gender.

For the one who moved thousands of miles away from their Christian family that had more interest in *deadnaming* them than showing them the love of the God they loved.

For the ones who cried in my arms after I gave seminars on the topic of sexual and gender identity, and expressed the fear they had over trying to walk through their identity with their Church family and pastors.

For the child who lived as a closet gay, instead of finding the support he needed within his Church and family.

For the one who confessed to me that he had to hide his testimony of coming to know Christ as it involved coming out about his transition because his Church told him if he shared about his journey he could no longer serve or attend.

For the ones who have felt a pang of fear when I shared my profession as a pastor because of past hurts in their lives.

For the Gay Village in British Colombia, Canada that suffered yet another hurt on August 24th, 2020, when a pastor chose to defend the Gospel from sinners by breaking the leg of a prominent Sportscaster who challenged his perception of God's love.

For every individual who felt *less than*, because we—*like slavers*—have used the Gospel to justify our actions.

I write for you.

Abbreviations

AJPH	American Journal of Public Health
EHRT	Egale Human Rights Trust.
FT	First Things
JAAR	Journal of the American Academy of Religion
JHS	Journal of the History of Sexuality
JRE	Journal of Religious Ethics
JRH	Journal of Religion and Health
JSSR	Journal for the Scientific Study of Religion
LT	Labour/Le Travail
OCASI	Ontario Council of Agencies Serving Immigrants.
ODCC	Oxford Dictionary of the Christian Church
OHRC	Ontario Human Rights Commission.
PP	Pastoral Psychology
TCC	The Christian Century
TNIB	The New Interpreter's Bible

Introduction

In preparing to write this book, I have often thought of my friends and family members who have experienced the hate and pain that the church has offered them. I have thought of the hurt they have experienced for which I too am responsible. I have thought of what they see when they see an image of Christ, or a picture of the church. It isn't the love we hope for them to see. How could it be love and hope when all we have offered is more hatred, hurt, and judgement?

This has led me to the conclusion that *how we minister matters*. If it didn't, the way that the church has been perceived by our culture would not be as negative as it currently stands. Those in the culture around us have seen our choices, our actions, and our reactions—and many have chosen to become people of faith, but not people of church. Those who live on the east coast of Canada are more likely to experience a general fondness for the church than what you may experience as a reaction in Toronto, Vancouver, Ottawa, or in many of our First Nations communities. Our time of ministry in the US taught my family that this is not a unique circumstance. In some places, to say, *"I go to church"* immediately places you within a negative, radical, exclusionist group.

How do we minister effectively in the ever-changing tides of culture? How we minister matters—especially to those who have already been hurt by the church—whether in the distant or recent past. Instead of ministering out of love and compassion, the church has been often ministering out of a deep-rooted fear. In total honesty, this fear is not that Christ will not triumph, but that the liberties found in the dominance of Christendom will disappear. This may seem like a negative event; however, we must remember that Christendom was not necessarily a positive event for the church. The integrity of the Gospel message has been hurt by the way we have wielded the power we have been given.

What has brought us to administer hatred instead of allowing the balm of the Holy Spirit's tender care to define our actions? We need to renew our Christian commitment to social responsibility and justice as a primary focus of the church. As such, our churches must begin to question the practices and visions which we hold most important in our community. Is our ministry truly inclusive to all who would seek to find solace at the feet of Christ?

In terms of *how* the church should respond to issues of Sexual & Gender Identity, there must be a *united* answer given. This important step may seem impossible in many regards, as the topic is so widely debated both in and outside of the church. However, without solidarity in at least treatment of those who identify themselves as a member of the Queer community the church will be ineffective.

As you begin this book, I want to warn you that I am not here to tell you what you need to believe about sexual or gender identity. I am not writing this book to promote either a liberal position or a conservative one on the matter of identity and sin. If you are looking for a book to help you justify a particular position, please look elsewhere.

What I promise to offer you in this book is a place to consider how to love others as an ally—even if you do not agree on matters of sexual and gender identity. My intent is to create a space in which we can have real discussions about what God's kingdom and community look like. Depending on your position on matters of identity, you may translate my recommendations differently than other readers, and that's okay. The goal is to become a community with one another.

There are three main positions that must be considered for a Christian to take in response to non-binary practices. These perspectives of the church on Queer sexual activity are: Celibacy;

Marital, Covenant or Equal-Partnership; and Casual Intimacy. Celibacy promotes complete restriction of Queer individuals from sexual relationships. Martial, Covenant and Equal-partnership would describe Queer relationships as "an acceptable lifestyle for Christians provided the partners are equal-status, consenting adults and the relationship is one of a monogamous, covenant and lasting kind."[1] Casual relationships would include "any member of society provided it involves adults . . . not simply within covenant relationships."[2]

Regardless of whether a person might adopt a philosophy of full acceptance, or full denial of Queer practices as God-honouring, one trait must remain in their response: *inclusion.* Without inclusive language and practice, the church does not live up to the higher calling that it has been given. Every individual has the right to be included in our communities.

Our differences in tradition and the interpretation of Scripture as denominations does not mean that one position is innately more holy or God-honouring than others. A note must here be taken from Feminist theology, there must be a "theological movement of various strands which are united in a determination to secure change for the better in terms of social justice."[3] In this fallen world, it is our *collective* Christian responsibility to ensure that our commitment to social justice and the inclusion of all people into God's kingdom remains a trademark.

In the words of F.E.D. Schleiermacher, while "no particular form of fellowship is here definitely asserted or excluded; every form, perfect or imperfect, that has ever been or that may yet appear, is included."[4] While he spoke to the church and the practices as a whole, his words are timely and appropriate on this issue as well. Does our Christian commitment to social justice and transformation stop at matters of sexual identity?

---

1. Webb, *Slaves, Women and Homosexuals*, 28.

2. Webb, *Slaves, Women and Homosexuals*, 28.

3. ODCC, "Feminist Theology," 607.

4. Schleiermacher, *Christian Faith*, 525–528.

The "religion of Jesus makes the love-ethic central."[5] Whether a Christian remains supportive, indifferent, or against particular gender/sexual expressions, this ethic of inclusive love is very clear: "a man must love his neighbour directly, clearly, permitting no barriers between."[6] Nothing can separate humanity from the love of God, and in likeness to the love that God offers us, humanity should let nothing hinder holistic inclusion.

To do so out of human strength or desire is impossible, but to love one another inclusively is possible in Christ. In his treatise, *Life Together,* Dietrich Bonhoeffer explains the unique natures of the two kinds of love. "Human love produces human subjection, dependence, constraint; spiritual love creates *freedom* of brethren under the Word. . .the life or death of a Christian community is determined by whether it achieves sober wisdom on this point."[7] To counter the specific pitfalls that the church has long fallen prey to, we must be the inclusive and loving body of Christ.

I do not write these things to shame you. I am in this period of learning and growth with you. My intent is to give us tools as the church—as the body of Christ—so that we can minister more effectively to our communities. I hope to equip us so that we can reclaim the positive image of Christ's truth & love that we are meant to carry as Christ's ambassadors. May we learn to offer the hope of transformation and love, and may it be our response to those around us. Hatred, hurt, and judgement have no place in the church—it is time to pull the weeds.

5. Thurman, *Jesus and the Disinherited,* 79.

6. Thurman, *Jesus and the Disinherited,* 79.

7. Bonhoeffer, *Life Together,* 37.

PART ONE

*Setting the Stage for
Informed Ministries*

CHAPTER 1

Sexual Identity and the Church

A Historical View of Sexual Identity and the Church

Church, State, and Matters of Sexual Identity

Moral values within North American families and relationships have been deeply influenced by the role of the church in our communities. Families seeking to hold celebrations of new life and marriages look to the church out of tradition and expectation. As two nations founded by the former citizens of Christian nations, we have experienced a great leisure in the general perception of the church.

North American churches are unilaterally facing changes in their role of social governance. There is a space between Canadian and American values that must be addressed as we set the tone for our discussion. The expected moral compass of the church continues to be a relatively consistent pattern within much of the United States, but the standard in Canada has long since ventured from this traditional and expected role of the church. In Canada, other religions have stepped into the forefront of our communities, and it is no longer only our voice in the vacuum of spiritual care. This was most notable during the early days of the Coronavirus pandemic when it was not Christians, but Sikhs who rose to the challenge and fed thousands in Toronto who had no income to support themselves or their families.

Two major differences exist between the Canadian and American relationships of church and state. In addressing the nature of their interactions in each country, it can primarily be noted that unlike the Unites States, Canada was not founded on religious principles, but rather on the independent values of diversity, freedom, and equality. This intrinsic separation of church and state has come more naturally in Canada than what is currently happening in the United States. This fundamental difference likely contributes to the impression that Canada is far more progressive or liberal as a nation.

The second fundamental difference that exists between these two North American nations is the sense of social responsibility that is inherent in Canadian culture—a practice which is often mis-identified as socialist. While the broader American culture venerates heritage, the broader Canadian culture embraces culpability and makes reparations for the past atrocities that have been committed in the name of diversity, freedom, and equality.

These differences are not shown to paint one nation as a utopian society—clearly that would not be a vision of reality. Instead, I simply mean to highlight the common practice that exists in each nation within each context of ministry. More importantly, this comparison helps us to identify the kind of responses that we must address moving forward in our ministries to communities which we have isolated and ostracized because of their sexual or gender identities.

History is not without examples that can be applied to the current question of sexuality and the church. Dr. William Webb, among other scholars, has suggested that issues of sexual identity should be compared scripturally and socially to the historical issues of slavery and women's rights.[1] These may seem to be strange

---

1. Webb, *Slaves, Women, and Homosexuals,* 68.

connections to make, but when we look at their progressions or patterns of teaching within Scripture, they can foster our approach to sexual and gender identity.

This approach can be summarized in one short statement as expressed in "Being Biblical? Slavery, Sexuality and the Inclusive Community." Therein, Rev. Dr. Richard Burridge proposed that "the abolition controversy two hundred years ago parallels our current crisis between those who want to be biblically upholding the tradition and those who are 'inclusive.'"[2] Simply stated, there is a historical tension that exists between those who desire to preach the hard truth of Scripture, and those who desire to offer the love of God.

Our politics, economics, and social standards are a further evidence of differentiating historical practices of Canada and the United States. Historically, Canada has been more intrinsically tied to liberty by inclusion—fostering freedom through the work of the Underground Railroad and ultimately creating the internationally used *Charter of Human Rights and Freedoms*. In contrast, American culture primarily enacts liberty through independence.

Historically the conditions of gender equality, sexual identity or practices, and slavery have worsened at the hands of those who sought to weaponize Scripture for the purpose of developing hateful opinions and practices. Examples taken from history show us that the use of apartheid or segregation was amplified by scriptural abuses. The exclusion of Black individuals in the nineteenth and twentieth centuries was so great that it led to their development of a separate identity or ecclesiology. Black Christians did not accept the way that the privileged, Anglo-Saxon Christians interpreted Scriptures in the nineteenth century, but still retained the value of the holy book.[3] Many women also distanced themselves from male-dominant interpretations of the past and began to approach Scripture with a greater hope for equality.[4]

---

2. Burridge, "Being Biblical?" 23.

3. Massey, *Reading the Bible*, 157.

4. Osiek, "Reading the Bible," 182.

This has, in practice, been an extension of our Christian commitment to holiness and social justice. Under the care of recent leadership, many denominations have come a long way from the days of the Civil Rights Movement when we were "revivalists, yes; reformers, no."[5] We are moving in the right direction, but the work is not yet done.

Terrorism, beatings, and murders have all been justified by the mistreatment of Scripture. Our culture is guilty of kindred acts based on which gender (or genders) attend romantic dates or weddings. While these acts may appear to be historically far more isolated compared to visible violence against women or people of color, it is likely due to a lack of media coverage rather than actual frequency.

A discussion and investigation on the matter, written by Fred Fejes, describes that while the term *homosexual* was not often included in the daily news, terms such as *sexual deviants, sodomizers,* and *perverts* were casually used in the twentieth century—often to amplify fear.[6] It is important to note here that while the global church has appeared to take a rather silent or traditional approach to the conversation on homosexuality, this was not always so. Fejes makes this important ecclesiastical distinction in his case study of the homosexual controversy in Miami in the twentieth century.

As a distinct example of recorded conflict, many in Miami sought to silence and eradicate those whom they referred to as deviants. In the face of this suppression, one church stood up and fought for legal freedoms for individuals who had long been considered criminals. Through an open forum series of discussions they hosted local community members to engage in a conversation about what true community looked like. They even "argued for changes in laws that [had previously] criminalized [homosexual practices]."[7] This church did not believe that there was biblical support for non-heterosexual practices or unions, but they still openly

---

5. Black and Drury, *Story of the Wesleyan Church*, loc. 2398 of 7078.

6. Fejes, "Murder, Perversion," 306–47.

7. Fejes, "Murder, Perversion," 324.

combatted the laws which criminalized a lifestyle or sexual procliv-
ity that was not their own.

This strong view of transformation theology from within the
church stood in the face of the homophobic citizens of Miami who
pressured the mayor and police chief to ameliorate the local situation by beating individuals for their aberrant sexual identity and
"recognize the abnormal in their children."[8] Their understanding of
the matter may not have been fully informed, but the church acted
within what they understood biologically, culturally, and biblically.
In this particular case, the church took a redemptive stand for the
right that human beings ought to be treated with dignity and re-
spect, regardless of their personal lives or propensities. This church
stood firm in their commitment to showing the love of God by de-
weaponizing Scripture.

Canadian churches also played an early role in decriminal-
ization of homosexual practices. In 1964, Arnold Peters, a young
politician for the New Democratic Party and member of the Canadian Council on Religion and the Homosexual (CCRH) was among
the first to propose homosexual law reforms in Parliament. While
his original proposal did not pass, it is important to note that the
CCRH was a council supported both officially and unofficially by
many churches—including the Anglican Church and the Roman
Catholic Church.[9]

Social and Political Context

In fairness the culture of the twentieth century both inside and
outside the church was deeply saturated by the events that shaped
the generation. This was a generation that had witnessed two global
scale wars, and felt that they were on the cusp of further conflict
when the initial, large-scale talks of homosexuality came to the
forefront. This period of fear was a time when any abnormalities or
divergences from the normative social pattern were seen as weaknesses, and weaknesses could not be tolerated.

8. Fejes, "Murder, Perversion," 331.

9. Kinsman, *Wolfenden in Canada*, 191–92.

During the Cold War era, the United States and Canada actively developed distinct programs of identifying, isolating, and removing homosexuals and people who otherwise diverged from the ideal White, cisgender, heterosexual standard from positions of power. In the United States, there remained a sense of openness to the public in these hearings, perhaps to help fuel the fear or alienation of practices perceived as abnormal and dangerous in the same way that some nations have historically used public punishments or executions.

In stark contrast to American methodology, "proceedings in Canada were much less public and visible."[10] Gary Kinsman describes that due to the secrecy of the issue in Canada, there would have been "no possibility for independent review" of the trials that took place.[11] With this as a common practice in Canada, many of the sins of Canadian history—especially those against our own citizens—are still only coming to light. People who diverged from what was considered as normative standards simply disappeared.

While limited examples of support and inclusion existed, the North American church primarily took one of two positions: they remained passive or allowed themselves to be swept into the hysteria that surrounded the vulnerability of the issue. When hysteria over the culture met the hardline conservative position in the early years of the twentieth century, homosexuality became "a symbol for . . . evil."[12] This being said, this apparent symbol for evil worked in a multifaceted manner, and could reflect not only the evil of homosexuals, but also the goodness of Christians. Homosexual evangelism became more focused on how it was considered a "test of . . . Christian character" than on ministering to the community.[13]

10. Kinsman, "'Character Weaknesses,'" 141.

11. Kinsman, "'Character Weaknesses,'" 141.

12. Dadisman, *Roots of Hate*, 25.

13. Dadisman, *Roots of Hate*, 25.

Repercussions of Church Silence
towards Sex and Sexuality

The church must be willing to build bridges that enable the creation of a holistic environment and healthy responses to the needs of others. This progression into a society of inclusion will not be a "new form of church" but rather a "network of communion of Churches."[14] The past cannot be changed, but should the church begin decisive, positive action now, there remains hope for redemption and inclusion.

In Canadian culture, there exists the natural, communal longing for reparations and apologies. In response to this national sense of need, Canadian ministers—both pastors and believers—must consider how their local church should function within the larger community. Likewise, if the "American Dream" truly offers liberty by individual rights and freedoms, do all people qualify?

American and Canadian churches must accept that there is hard work to be done in rebuilding bridges we have burned. Our voice has not been communicating the gospel to all peoples and all nations. We hide our vague guidelines, incomplete position statements, and shallow directives on our church websites and in our dusty church handbooks. We have been quick to protest and slow to offer support for individuals in need because of their sexual or gender identity. The only witness of love towards the ostracized has been the voices of the secular community as they preach the message of hope we have lost sight of in our fear.

Many were angered by the words of Macklemore and Ryan Lewis when they debuted the song "Same Love." I remember hearing Christian friends, family, and pastors lamenting that an open celebration of Queer marriage was on the radio. I wept too, but not for the same reasons. I wept tears of culpability because of the words at the end of the song which call the church into account. I realized that I, as a minister, had been responsible for teaching words that were not anointed by God. I spoke words that, instead of calling the little children to come to him, offered the poison of fear that was seeping into our holy water.

14. Zizioulas, *Being as Communion*, 257–59.

As a priesthood that has said extraordinarily little about matters of sexual identity, it is worth our deep consideration to determine what will be our first step. In what voice and manner will we present ourselves—and more importantly—in what manner will we present the hope of Jesus Christ to the world? If we act without consideration of the Christian role in past discriminations, we may ultimately lose our opportunity to reach others for Christ.

CHAPTER 2

Transforming Our Vision of Responsibility

Social Justice and the Practice of Inclusionary Ministries

A Wesleyan Perspective of Transformation and Heritage of Social Justice

In the shift of the global church from social centerpiece to the fringes of society, the process of evangelism and discipleship has become stagnant. This is not to say that the global church has not been trying to reach out, but rather to say that we have been working too hard in the wrong directions. As a result, the church has been deeply affected by gender traditionalism, and restricted views of the roles of men and women.

Even denominations that support women in ministry are not exempt from this pervading idea. Gender role traditionalism and Complementarian beliefs do not only harm our ability to enable men and women to serve in their full capacity as leaders, but they also harm our perception of those who do not fit within traditional identity patterns. As a result, those within the church are more likely to think that our responsibility is to teach people that they are wrong than to love them.[1] *That's not our role, that's our intrusion on the role of the Holy Spirit.*

Although we are affected by these harmful views, there are patterns through which we can emerge as faithful ministers. We have a strong faith heritage on which we stand that show our commitment to identifying issues of social justice and supporting those most in need. Many Christians have worked to abolish slavery, give women the right to vote, ordain women for ministry, and fight against human trafficking. Our heritage of social justice gives hope, but it also makes us culpable. If we turn a blind eye to the needs of the Queer community, we are doing little more than the Jewish leaders who would rather ask, "And who is my neighbor?" (Luke 10:29b) than help them. If we are truly living by Mic 6:8, then we are responsible to care for God's Queer children too.

As an example, the Wesleyan Church practices and presents faith as an opportunity for all people to believe, belong, and become. When we break down evangelism and discipleship into these parts, it is much easier to see where and how we can support one another—regardless of our race, gender, or identity. This method has all the right parts, but in order to most effectively reach those whom we have ostracized—intentionally or incidentally—we must at least situationally reorder the approach.

It was sitting at the feet of Jesus that gave people the opportunity to believe in him. Jesus first welcomed all as children of God, and then invited them to transformational belief. In the context of ministering to those who have been ostracized from the faith, we must create a space in which all can find a sense of belonging so that some can find belief.

We need to ask ourselves what our churches look like now, and whether we are invitational to all individuals. Are we ministering at status quo? Or are we readily seeking to create space for the orphans and widows of the faith to find their way back home?

---

1. Whitehead, *Male and Female*, 479–496.

My son, Tristan, loves to sing when we read Bible stories together. Of course, this means that my husband and I pull out the songs that we learned in Sunday school as kids. However, we have adjusted some of these songs to engage our hearts in inclusion—as we are called to do by Christ. Rather than singing a song that could be perceived as racially charged, we have changed the lyrics of classic song "Jesus Loves the Little Children" from "Red, Brown, Yellow, Black, and White" to "Every Person, Every Life."

This is not a compromise of our faith pattern. In creating space for all people to come and participate in faith, we remove the expectations that may prevent others from joining our congregations and families. In creating space, we are simply extending the grace and love of Christ to those who are not in relationship with him.

Apologies before Apologetics

We must acknowledge the need for the church to bridge divides of culture and personal value. We, as the church, stand at the precipice of a valuation divide that has the potential to undermine anything that we might say to help others discern their identity in Christ. In order to continue efforts in ministry in this climate, we must be ready to submit ourselves humbly within our communities.

In the volatile confrontation of Mary over the death of her brother, Lazarus, "Jesus began to weep" (John 11:35). Jesus' response to her allowed for a genuine and shared experience in grief with one another. This is the response of an individual who listens to the careful prompting of the Holy Spirit in the face on grief and pain (John 11:33). When we offer our apologies and share our grief for the silence of our past towards the needs of those in sexual and gender diverse lifestyles, it breaks down the barricades of hatred that we have helped build between church and the Queer community.

It is important that we confess and admit that wrongdoing has occurred in our actions and inactions. Admitting that maltreatment has occurred does not mean a softening of our scriptural position—only a softening of our hearts to become more like Christ.

Hatred has no place in the gospel, and the removal of this sin of pride begins in compassionate and humble grief.

It should be noted that our positive actions of reconciliation will not erase hatred from the realm of possibility. There will always be those individuals who choose not to agree or align with our practices, beliefs, etc. Regardless, we must strive to not aggravate the situation by ignoring past hurts and present mistreatments.

Recognizing Where We Can Help— Developing Awareness of Queer Needs

Our process of creating space for members of the Queer community within our churches begins with recognizing their unique social and personal needs. It is important that we as ministers of the gospel educate ourselves by finding resources within our communities and online that can help us better understand how to support individuals. While there will be regional issues—things that are unique to your country, city, etc.—here are a few questions to begin addressing:

1. Does your church or business require people to identify their gender on your connect cards? Are your most active ministries—those you offer events or activities for—primarily gendered (women's and men's ministries)?
2. What is your bathroom situation? Do you offer single stall bathrooms or gendered multi-stall bathrooms?
3. Does your liturgy or communications include all of God's children?
4. What do you *honestly* know about Queer culture?

Members of the Queer community may find it difficult to find their place within your community if your focus is inadvertently on traditional genders. This discomfort may stem from a fear for personal safety, or other negative experiences. Solutions may include changing the traditional men's events that are masculine or women's events that are more traditionally feminine activities to ungendered events that are each open to all participants. As a tomboy married to an emotional man, even we who fall within the traditional paradigm for marriage would thank you for this change.

On connect cards, perhaps instead you could ask people to share their preferred pronoun with you on a blank line (with no suggested choices), so that you can help give them a sense of inclusion. This can create a much more welcoming atmosphere for individuals seeking to find a community. It also opens the door for communication by showing your awareness that not every person identifies themself in the same way. It may also be helpful to sign off on your emails with an added line below your name/credentials/title that says your preferred pronouns. For example:

> Final Greetings,
> Rev. Olivia Phillips
> The Name of My Workplace or Church/Position
> Titles/Degree
> She/Her (*preferred pronouns*)

Traditional gender roles can also negatively affect the layout of our physical spaces. If your local church or business has single occupant bathrooms, simply remove the male/female signs and you are all set. The pressure of being forced to choose one gendered restroom or another may be overwhelming—especially for those who are new in their experience of a particular gender identity. If you already have a facility with gendered washrooms, make it a priority to create space and comfort for all congregants. If you do not have the budget to completely replace your bathroom facilities with single or family occupancy stalls, perhaps your solution will be to build floor-to-ceiling stall enclosures—eliminating the chances of accidental exposure or *outing* a person. Privacy is something everyone could use a little more of in restrooms.

Do your services reflect the diversity of your community? Is Scripture presented holistically in your church—showing portions of the Old and New Testaments? Does your worship service reflect your desires to empower and offer the transforming love of God to all people? What does your leadership *look* like? In your promotional material, do you only focus on a traditional view of family—or do you include single parents and other representations of family? Members of the Queer community likewise seek to see the inclusion of all of God's children and fight for social justice. This common goal can create unity and offer a sense of inclusion to those who need it most.

If the only things you know about Queer culture come from Christian preachers or sitcoms, it is time to do a little homework. Learn about the genuine struggles of the Queer community that have led to their representation today. Do you know iconic members of the Queer community in your city, state/province, or country? Listen and learn—your ministry will be more informed and compassionate as a result.

Defining Sexualities and Genders— Informing the Church of Cultural Shifts

As a part of our responsibility, we must educate ourselves on matters of gender and sexual identity. Please bear in mind as you read the following definitions that culture is not stagnant. We should expect that these descriptions may rapidly change and grow as the culture of sexual identity is likewise changing and growing. Some of these definitions have not existed for long—as there has not always been safety in public expression. As this sense of safety in exploration grows, larger groups of people have begun to explore how their sexual and gender identity can be perceived and defined.

This section is included so that you may be equipped to recognize and offer support to each member of your local community. What matters most about these definitions to the church community is that they are at the forefront of our awareness as we speak about engaging with sexual identity in our context.

These are not intended to be weaponized, nor are they meant to be labels we can apply at *our will*. These definitions are meant to help us understand the context or lens through which others view their own sexual identity or gender experience. It is the responsibility of each Christian to stay informed about how to communicate within the parameters of culture in a manner that is appropriate and loving. If it helps you develop a mindset in which to frame this education, we are doing much the same work as a missionary who learns more about a foreign culture. We learn so that we can show love.

Comprehensive Glossary of Terms for Gender and Sex Identity and Expression[2]

Term	Definition	Cautions/Notes
Affirmed Gender	The gender with which an individual identifies or has transitioned socially to identify with. *See also* "Experienced Gender"	
Assigned Gender	This generally refers to the same concept as sex assigned at birth. *See also* "Birth-Assigned Gender" and "Gender Assigned at Birth (GAAB)"	Some individuals give the distinction between sex/gender and correspond this solely to cultural and legal categorization rather than a biological categorization.
Agender	An individual who does not identify or relate to any gender identity.	
All-gender space	A place which all genders may utilize.	For example, gender-neutral or gender-inclusive washrooms.
Ally	An individual who defends the rights and freedoms of marginalized communities to which they do not belong—and can be recognized as such by those within the marginalized communities in question.	

2. This comprehensive list has been informed by several medical and cultural resources.
EHRT, "Glossary of Terms." Egale Resources.
OCASI, "Glossary of Terms." OCASI: Positive Space Initiative.
OHRC, *Policy on Preventing Discrimination*, Appendix B.
Airton, *Gender: Your Guide*, 23–43.
Teich, *Transgender 101*, 1–13.

Ambisexual, -ity	An individual whose sexual orientation (state) is ambivalent or changing.	
Androgyny, Androgynous	An individual whose sex cannot (easily) be determined by their gender expression.	
Asexual, -ity	An individual who feels very little or no sexual desire in any notable amount towards another person—regardless of sex or gender identity. Asexuality can be seen as a spectrum and may even identify within a particular romantic orientation. An asexual person may build emotionally romantic relationships and long-lasting partnerships with other individuals.	
Attraction	The classification of an individual's sexual, physical, and emotional interest in another—often based on the sex and/or gender. *See also* "Sexual Orientation"	
"Be in the closet"	The act of concealing a sexual orientation or gender identity (may be passive, active, or forced).	
Bicuriosity, Bicurious	The state of an individual that is open or curious about sexual relations with person(s) whose sex differs from that of their typical sexual partners.	This term can be seen as disparaging or pejorative.
Bigender, Bi-gender	An individual that identifies as having two genders.	
Biological sex	Refers to the individual's biological status—male, female, or intersex. Indicators of Biological Sex can include: sex chromosomes, internal reproductive organs, and external genitalia.	Term can be sometimes considered disparaging or pejorative by Trans individuals.

Biphobia, Biphobic, Biphobe	Fear, hatred, or hostility towards individuals who identify as bisexual and the practice of bisexuality. This can be both individual and systemic in nature.	
Birth-Assigned Gender	This generally refers to the same concept as sex assigned at birth. *See also* "Assigned Gender" and "Gender Assigned At Birth (GAAB)"	Some individuals give the distinction between sex/gender and correspond this solely to cultural and legal categorization rather than a biological categorization.
Bisexual, -ity	Referring to an individual who is sexually attracted to people of their own and one other sex. The attraction of a bisexual person may not be equal in amounts and can be fluid.	
Cisgender	A person whose gender identity aligns with their sex assigned at birth.	
Cisnormative, -ity	An often implicit cultural or social framework in which all individuals are cisgender and this is the normative experience.	
Cissexism, Cisgenderism	Practice of discrimination against those who are not cisgender or align with cisnormative culture.	
Cissexuality	The state in which an individual's sex at birth aligns with their gender identity.	
"Come Out" "Coming Out"	The act of voluntarily revealing one's gender identity or sexual orientation. This can be a single event or a lifelong process.	
"Conceal" "Concealment"	The act of hiding one's gender identity or sexual orientation.	This can be an act committed out of fear for safety, insecurity, or other reasons entirely.

Cross-dresser, Cross-dressing	An individual who permanently or occasionally presents their gender expression as different from their typical gender identity.	These individuals do not generally identify as transgender.
Deadname	(Noun) This most often refers to the birth name of a transgender individual—which they no longer use. (Verb) This is also the term by which an individual refers to a trans individual by their name of birth.	To willfully *deadname* a person is considered extremely hateful. This is akin to rejecting the individual's chosen identity.
Demiboy Demi-boy Demiguy Demi-guy	An individual whose gender identity is partially male and partially another gender.	
Demigender Demi-gender	An individual whose gender identity is partially associated with a particular gender.	
Demigirl Demi-girl	An individual whose gender identity is partially female and partially another gender.	
Demisexual, -ity	An individual whose sexual attraction is only felt for another individual once a strong emotional bond has been formed.	
Detransition, -ing	The process in which an individual reverses previous transitional changes in order to reflect their gender assigned at birth.	There are social, medical, and legal aspects which affect detransitioning. Some individuals may only choose this process as a means of securing personal safety.
Diamoric	An individual who expresses a non-binary identity that experiences attraction to other individuals who are non-binary.	
Drag King	A woman (trans or cis-) that temporarily dresses in men's clothing and acts with exaggerated masculinity—often for performance.	This is not an indication of sexual orientation, nor of gender identity.

Drag Queen	A man (trans or cis-) who temporarily dresses in women's clothing and acts with exaggerated femininity—often for performance.	This is not an indication of sexual orientation, nor of gender identity.
Dyadic Female	An individual easily categorized as male at birth due to the presence of the following biological characteristics: external penis, external testes, high levels of testosterone, and XY chromosomes.	
Dyadic Male	An individual easily categorized as female at birth due to the presence of the following biological characteristics: external vagina, internal uterus/ovaries, high levels of estrogen, and XX chromosomes.	
Experienced Gender	The gender with which an individual identifies. *See also* "Affirmed Gender"	
Feminine	A word to describe a behavior, trait, or style of expression that has cultural associations with *womanhood*. The standards of what is deemed feminine, are not universal, but are formed uniquely within cultures.	
Female Same-sex Parenting	A family in which the parents are both female and lesbian. *See also* "Lesbian Parenting"	
Female to Male (FTM) (F2M)	A trans individual who was born in a body assigned female at birth and transitions to identify as male	Do not use this term to identify an individual unless they self-identify with it, as it can be perceived as offensive.
Found Family	This term refers to the family collected/adopted by individuals who have created a family with other members of the Queer community. *See also* "Gay Family," "Lesbian Family," *and* "Queer Family"	

Gay	An individual who is sexually attracted to people who align with the same sex as them. Typically refers to men, but can also refer to other genders. *See also* "Homosexual, -ity"	
Gay Family	A family in which the parents are of the same-sex. This term can also refer to the family collected/adopted by individuals who have created a family with other members of the Queer community. *See also* "Found Family," "Lesbian Family," and "Queer Family"	
Gay Father Family	A family in which the parents identify as men.	
Gay Parenting	A family in which the parents identity as gay.	
Gender	An individual's status in society as a man, woman, or non-binary person. While "sex" refers to an individual's physical characteristics, gender includes the expectations, stereotypes, actions, and roles linked to a particular sex. As such, concepts of gender can vary depending on culture, etc. Gender can also refer to the differences and relations between sexes that are learned through social context to determine position and status.	

Gender Affirming Surgery (GAS)	A surgery which modifies an individual's sexual anatomical characteristics to align with their gender identity. This process is often broken into two major categories of transition: top surgery (to allow the individual to reflect their chosen gender in the appearance of breasts/facial reconstruction), and bottom surgery (primarily to allow external sexual organs to reflection the individual's chosen gender).	Also known as: Gender Confirmation Surgery/ Gender Confirming Surgery (GCS), Sexual Reassignment Surgery (SRS), or Sex Change Surgery (SCS).
Gender and Sexual Diversity (GSD)	A term considered more inclusive than LGBT as it does not specify any particular genders or sexual orientations.	
Gender and Sexual Minorities (GSM)	A term considered more inclusive than LGBT as it includes all people whose identity differs sexually or in gender from the majority of society.	
Gender Assigned At Birth (GAAB)	This generally refers to the same concept as sex assigned at birth. *See also* "Birth-Assigned Gender" and "Assigned Gender"	Some individuals give the distinction between sex/gender and correspond this solely to cultural and legal categorization rather than a biological categorization.
Gender Balance	Balance between sexes	
Gender Bending	The act of blurring the boundaries between genders	

Gender Binary, -ism	The idea that gender is separated into two fixed and closed categories, man and woman, and that it cannot be a variety of identities and expressions.	While Scripture may inform Christians of the ideal gender experience as binary, the act of limiting one's view of experienced gender as binary can deny the identities, and realities of individuals.
Gender-Blind, Genderblind	The lack of distinction between genders by an individual	
Gender Conforming, -ity	The act of becoming consistent with what is culturally associated with one's own sex or gender assigned at birth.	This usually refers to gender expression—in behavior, clothing, and voice inflection, etc.
Gender Differences	The distinctions between sexes.	
Gender Dysphoria	A condition in which an individual experiences persistent discomfort and/or distress due to a mismatch between their gender identity and the sex they were assigned at birth.	
Gendered	The organization or separation by categories or associations of gender.	This term is used of places, occupations, or objects rather than individuals.
Gender Equality	The belief that all individuals, regardless of their gender, are free to develop their personal abilities and make choices without the limitations set by stereotypes, rigid gender roles, and prejudices, and that different behaviours, aspirations, and needs of all individuals are considered, valued, and favoured equally.	

Gender Equity	The fair treatment of all individuals, according to their respective needs.	While treatment can be different for each individual, it must remain equivalent in rights, benefits, obligations, and opportunities.
Gender Expressions	The appearance or acts typically associated with a gender.	This is not necessarily associated with an individual's gender identity.
Gender Fluid Gender-Fluid	An individual whose gender identity or expression changes or shifts along the gender spectrum.	
Gender Identity	An individual's internal, deeply experienced sense of gender—this may or may not align with their sex assigned at birth.	This may not be visible and may not be related to an individual's sexual orientation.
Gender-Inclusive Pronouns	Personal pronouns which refer to an individual without associating a gender to them.	
Gender-non-conforming	Deviation from that which is expected culturally or socially from sex assigned at birth or binary framework for gender.	Typically, this is witnessed in one's gender expression.
Gender Norm	The roles, behaviours, activities, and attributes constructed and deemed socially and culturally appropriate for each gender.	
Gender Parity	Equal contributions by the sexes to every dimension of life—both private and public.	
Genderqueer	An individual who challenges social and cultural norms with their identity, expression, and sexual practices.	
Gender Role	Behaviours traditionally associated with one's gender.	
Graysexual Gray-sexual Greysexual Grey-sexual, -ity	An individual who rarely feels sexual attraction.	

Hermaphrodite	An individual whose primary characteristics of sex at birth do not meet criteria for either the male or female sex. As a term, it does not refer to sexual orientation or gender identity.	This term is considered offensive, and should not be applied to humans.
Heteroflexible,—ility	A heterosexual individual who may occasionally be attracted to a person of the same sex	This term can be seen as pejorative and disparaging.
Heteronormative, -ity	A cultural or social framework, often implicit, wherein all human beings are heterosexual, and this is the norm.	The practice of heteronormativity often leads to the marginalization of sexual minorities either by dismissing them, by presenting a favourable bias towards heterosexual people, or both.
Heterosexism	Prejudice expressed against those whose orientation differs from heterosexuality	
Hijra	This is a South Asian term that denotes a third gender category reserved for those who are male assigned at birth (or intersex), but adopt qualities and mannerisms of the female gender.	Hijras often have a separated community and serve ceremonial roles in South Asian culture.
Homoflexible, -ility	A homosexual individual who may occasionally be attracted to a person of the opposite sex	This term can be seen as pejorative
Homonormativity	Cultural or social frameworks which transpose the standards of heteronormative standards on gender and sexual minorities.	For example: traditional forms of marriage/roles in Queer communities
Homophobia, -ic	Fear, Hatred, Hostility, and/or Prejudices towards homosexuals and the practices of homosexuality	
Homosexual, -ity	An individual who is sexually attracted to someone of their own sex	

Intersection-ality	The concept that an individual may face certain oppressions while also receiving privileges and opportunities.	For example: a Portuguese Lesbian Muslim may face racism, xenophobia, homophobia, Islamophobia, and sexism, but have privileges that a trans person or someone with a disability may not have.
Intersex, -uality	An individual whose primary characteristics of sex at birth do not meet criteria for either the male or female sex. It may be represented by a misalignment of hormones to genitalia or the presentation of genitalia in a manner that is not easily identified as one sex or another. These circumstances occur in 1 out of 1500 births.	As a term, it does not refer to sexual orientation or gender identity.

This term can also mean the positive, non-pathological self-image of an intersex individual. |
| Lesbian, -ism | A female who experiences sexual attraction to other women. | |
| Lesbian Family | The family collected/adopted by Lesbian individuals who have created a family with other members of the Queer—or specifically Lesbian community.

See also "Found Family," "Gay Family," and "Queer Family" | |
Lesbian Parenting	A family whose parents are individuals that identify as lesbian.	
LGBT	An acronym which stands for: Lesbian, Gay, Bisexual, and Trans	
LGBTQ	An acronym which stands for: Lesbian, Gay, Bisexual, Trans, and Queer/Questioning	
LGBTQ+	An acronym which stands for: Lesbian, Gay, Bisexual, Trans, Queer/Questioning, and Others	

LGBTQ2S	An acronym which stands for: Lesbian, Gay, Bisexual, Trans, Queer/Questioning, and Two-Spirit	
LGBTQIA+	An acronym which stands for: Lesbian, Gay, Bisexual, Trans, Queer/Questioning, Intersex, Asexual, and Others	
Male Same-sex Parenting	A family in which the parents identify as men.	
Masculine	A word to describe a behavior, trait, or style of expression that has cultural associations with *manhood*. The standards of what is deemed masculine, are not universal, but are formed uniquely within cultures.	
Misgender, -ing	The act of accidentally or intentionally incorrectly identifying or attributing an individual's gender.	This can occur in choices of pronouns, words, agreements or forms of address which do not correctly align with or reflect an individual's gender identity.
Monosexism	A framework in which social and cultural constructs create an implicit norm in which sexual attraction is solely homosexual.	This practice leads to the marginalization of those who are diversely attracted sexually.
Monosexual, -ity	An individual who is solely same-sex attracted	
Male-To-Female (MTF) (M2F)	A trans individual who was born in a body assigned male at birth and transitions to identify as female	Do not use this term to identify an individual unless they self-identify with it, as it can be perceived as offensive.
Multigender Multi-gender	An individual who identifies as having more than one gender	

Muxe (pronounced Moo-shays)	A culturally recognized third gender in the Mexican State of Oaxaca. Like Hijra's, they are typically born male and present with a female gender expression.	
Non-binary	An individual whose gender identity does not align with a binary understanding of gender—i.e., male and female Individuals who are non-binary may redefine gender, or decline the construct of a gender identity altogether	
"Out" "Outing"	The act of exposing an individual's sexual orientation or gender identity without the express permission of the individual.	This can also be a description of one's identity status—an individual who is "out." Can describe those who have chosen to "*Come Out*" voluntarily.
Pangender	An individual who identifies with all genders which are culturally available to them	
Pansexual,-ity	An individual whose sexual attraction is another individual regardless of their gender	
Passing	The act of hiding one's gender or sexual identity. This practice is often used to offer safety to individuals who may not be welcome in certain situations or places.	For example: an individual visiting a church or other gathering that may have a reputation for a less-than-welcoming atmosphere may choose to "pass" as a gender or sexual identity which is not their chosen, but is less likely to merit hate.
Perceived Gender Identity	The act of assuming an individual's gender identity without knowing their true gender identity. Often tied to stereotypes related to gender expression.	For example: what a transgender man *should* look like.

Perceived Sexual Orientation	The act of assuming an individual's sexual orientation without knowing their true sexual orientation. Often tied to stereotypes related to gender expression.	For example: what a lesbian woman *should* look like.
Polysexual, -ity	An individual who is sexually attracted to people of several genders.	
Preferred Gender Pronoun	A personal pronoun chosen by a person that matches their gender identity. This is a matter of identity rather than a mere preference for individuals.	
Protected Grounds	Categories of social identity or experience that have historically been the basis for disproportionate levels of disadvantage and discrimination.	Categories protected by the Ontario Human Rights Code include: Age, Ancestry, Colour, Race, Citizenship, Ethnic Origin, Place of Origin, Creed, Disability, Family Status, Marital Status (including single status), Gender Identity, Gender Expression, Receipt of Public Assistance (in housing only), Record of Offences (in employment only), Sex (including pregnancy and breastfeeding), Sexual Orientation

Queer	An individual (or community) whose sexual orientation or gender identity differs from the normative binary vision of gender and sexuality.	While this term was once considered derogatory, and can still be used in that way, this term has been reappropriated by gender and sexual minorities in an attempt to transform it from an insult into a symbol of freedom. When used as a broad descriptor, this term should be capitalized.
Queer Family	This term refers to the family collected/adopted by individuals who have created a family with other members of the Queer community. *See also* "Found Family," "Gay Family," and "Lesbian Family"	
Queerphobia, -ic	Fear, Hatred, Hostility, and/or Prejudices towards Queer individuals and their sexual practices	
Questioning	An individual who is uncertain of their own gender identity or sexual orientation. This may be a longstanding status or a period of decision making. This often reflects a process in which an individual reconciles three particular pieces of information: 1. Feelings of Attraction/expressions of Gender 2. Language available to utilize as a framework for those feelings/ expressions 3. The sense an individual has of how their expression and identity will impact their social interactions	

Sex	The label of male, female, intersex, or in transition. Typically, assigned based on a reading of an individual's sexual and reproductive anatomy.	How an individual identifies their gender or chooses to express such may not have any relation to their sex.
Self-identification Self-identified	The manner in which an individual chooses to describe their gender identity or sexual orientation	
Sex Assigned At Birth (SAAB)	An individual's sex as based on primary physical characteristics at birth.	Generally, this is the same concept as gender assigned at birth. However, others limit SAAB solely to the physical or biological characteristics.
Sexual Diversity	The spectrum of expression of an individual's sexual attraction, behavior, identity, and orientation.	
Sexual Minority	A group or individual whose sexual orientation is not in the majority of expression	
Sexual Orientation	An individual's sexual attraction—i.e., asexuality, bisexuality, heterosexuality, homosexuality, pansexuality, etc. See also "Attraction"	
Sworn Virgin	A Balkan/Albanian term that typically indicates an individual who was assigned female at birth and traditionally swears a lifelong vow of celibacy and lives their life as a male in their gender expression. This is considered to be a third gender category.	
Third Gender	Many cultures include a category of gender expression to include individuals who express and identify themselves beyond the bounds of binary gender.	For example: Muxes, Two-Spirit, Hijra, Sworn Virgins, etc.

Trans Transgender	A generic term meaning those who have transitioned from cisgender to a gender that does not align with their gender or sex assigned at birth. The transition does not have to, but often includes medically supportive treatments, such as hormone therapy or surgical procedures. This can be seen as an umbrella term, although some individuals choose to identify themselves solely as trans or transgender.	Individuals who are transgender may choose not to identify as transgender, but rather as the gender to which they have transitioned.
Transgender Man Trans Man	An individual assigned female at birth who identify as male. *See also* "Female to Male (FTM/ F2M)"	
Transgender Woman Trans Woman	An individual assigned male at birth who identify as female. *See also* "Male to Female (MTF/ M2F)"	
Transition, -ing	The process by which an individual makes changes to reflect their experienced gender in their personhood. This may change an individual's physical appearance, name, and/or legal documents. It may include medical interventions, but the process is not mandatory to self-identify as a transgender individual.	There is no universal end-goal or endpoint to the transition of an individual. Each individual decides what meets their individual needs for transitioning. For example, some individuals may pursue full SRS, while others may only pursue hormone therapies in order to achieve their transition.
Transparental Family, Trans Parenting	A family in which at least one parent is a transgender person	
Transphobia, -ic	Fear, Hatred, Hostility, and/or Prejudices towards transgender individuals and their sexual practices	

Transsexual, -ity	An individual whose sex does not align with the sex they were assigned at birth. Generally, transsexuals will undertake steps to change their sex assigned at birth.	Transgender is the preferred term as *transsexual* can be pejorative and strongly medically connotated.
Trigender	An individual who identifies as having three genders	
Two-Spirit Two-Spirit-edness	An individual, typically North American Indigenous, who embodies both male and female spirits or whose gender identity or spiritual identity is not limited by male/female dichotomy.	A person who is not of Indigenous descent should not self-identify as a two-spirit person as it is deeply rooted in cultural understandings and complex histories.
Ungender, -ed, -ing	To remove the structure of organization or associations with gender.	Often this process is used in a discriminatory manner by cis-gender individuals to seek evidence that trans individuals are no longer living life with the sex they were assigned at birth.

CHAPTER 3

Approaching the Scriptures in Humility

Building a Scriptural Foundation of Truth

Identifying a Hermeneutic from Which to Work

In 1969, homosexuality was decriminalized in Canada. Sodomy laws which applied to the Queer community, while not fully enforced, were only repealed in thirty-six of the United States in 2002. In 2003, the first Canadian province legalized gay marriage, and by 2005 the whole country would recognize homosexual marriage. The United States followed suit and legalized gay marriage nationwide in 2015. Regardless of your comfort level with these changes, we must recognize that the cultural perception of Queer rights and freedoms has drastically changed in the last few decades.

To understand this cultural shift, it is important to take account of the thought patterns that led to and emerged from the change. In terms of cultural movements that directly affect the church, we must be responsible to take a detailed look at the hermeneutical practices and thought processes we hold as Christians.

Traditionally, there was little room for discussion on passages that were seen as closed topics—sexual and gender identity or roles were often at the top of this list. However, our recent shift from relying solely on liturgical interpretation to embracing cultural interpretations of Scripture has opened doors for increased dialogue of these subjects.

When an approach to the Scriptures is first developed or revisited, it is likely that a new understanding of the text will arise. The goal is not to cast all previous interpretations in a negative light, but simply to say that alternatives exist in scriptural interpretations. Since the time following the Middle Ages, hermeneutical or study practices have seen hundreds of changes—although many of these changes were very minute.[1]

The method that primarily brought about the changing views on sexuality and gender identity was the trend of investigating the culture surrounding the text comparatively. This trend began to flourish in the late nineteenth and early twentieth centuries, and we are still seeing growth in this movement.[2] Some scholars have suggested that this is a dangerous practice—which it can be without proper caution and balancing efforts. This shift in study is an important step in understanding the world that the Holy Book was written within.

This method is described most clearly in the works of Dr. William Webb, who calls his practice of scriptural exegesis the "XYZ Principle."[3] Each letter of his principle represents a particular aspect of his interpretational method. This hermeneutical study pattern allows the reader to focus first on the isolated words (Y), then the original culture (X), and then interpret how these parts communicate to an ultimate ethic (Z).[4]

Principles of interpretation such as Webb's are meant to keep the interpreter attuned both to the original culture and environment of Scripture, while developing an awareness of modern

---

1. Terry, *Biblical Hermeneutics*, 13–14.
2. Terry, *Biblical Hermeneutics*, 732.
3. Webb, *Slaves, Women and Homosexuals*, 33.
4. Webb, *Slaves, Women and Homosexuals*, 31.

culture. For this reason, this method of interpretation is categorized as a dynamic or "redemptive-movement hermeneutic."[5] While other methods may seek to understand the Scriptures in isolation, this method appears to have a desire for a greater understanding of why the text says what it does *for the purpose of engagement and application.*

On topics such as slavery, women's rights, or sexual/gender identity, it is especially important to look at the general movement of the cultural background in comparison to the general movement of the scriptural position. While the word of God is ultimately still seen as infallible, many scholars who support this hermeneutic would agree that there must be a distinction made "between kingdom values and cultural values within the biblical text."[6] Each of these three topics demand careful attention, and a misuse or misunderstanding of the background could hold disastrous options for application in the church.

If the church were to return to the use of a static hermeneutic for the interpretation of these passages, the results would be clear. Strictly static interpretations of Scripture can lead to readers interpreting the subjugation of women and the ownership of slaves as a normative, even biblical practice. Divergence from the limited view of monogamous heterosexual marriage between cisgender partners in sexual or gender identity would be rigorously dismissed as sinful.

Ultimately, there remains one question for interpreters to answer when taking a dynamic hermeneutical approach. "When rightly interpreted, [Scripture] leads to Christ."[7] As individuals, pastors, and churches, we must ask ourselves: *does my interpretation of Scripture lead to the transforming hope of Jesus Christ?*

Building from a Hermeneutic of Inclusion and Embrace:

To discuss a theology of approach and practice for sensitive subject matters, one must consider the hermeneutical impact that has

5. Webb, *Slaves, Women and Homosexuals*, 35.

6. Webb, *Slaves, Women and Homosexuals*, 23.

7. McGrath, *Passion for Truth*, 54.

been made over the last two centuries. With the rise of modernity, there have been unique challenges to face, and sexual identity fits intrinsically and seamlessly into this trend. While in many ways, modernity had a rhetoric of unrestrained individual freedom, the struggle for personal liberty in sexual and gender identity did not develop large-scale until the later years of the movement.

Many Christians fear that the church now faces a culture of post-modern ideologies. Personal opinions are akin to truth, and universal truth faces a degree of extinction. In Canadian and more liberal contexts, there is also a measure of difficulty in ministering in pre-Christian settings as immigration and globalization expand our experiences of culture and religion.

The practice of a dynamic hermeneutic will not give everyone the same interpretation of key passages on matters of sexuality and gender identity—no hermeneutic is capable of such a task. What it will do is help us recognize the gravity of our cultural and scriptural impressions and how important it is for us to rely on the Holy Spirit in our efforts of interpretation. Whether we ultimately view Scripture as supporting all individuals in their expressions of sexual and gender identity or embrace a more restricted perspective, we must embrace our neighbours as cherished children of God. We cannot sing that our neighbors will know our faith by our commitment to love on Sunday morning, and be unwilling to engage with them in community by lunchtime.

The Christian response to the LGBTQIA2S+ community could be crippling to the global church if not addressed in a manner that reflects the intentions of Scripture appropriately. Our commitment to truth and our intent to love are "never judged merely by doctrinal ideas, but more so by their social products, the quality of their communities, [and] their ability to nurture a tradition through multigenerational challenges."[8]

Questions of sexual and gender identity, despite the ungodly hopes of many believers, are not going to simply disappear from the pews of churches, lines of grocery stores, or daily workplaces. "It is necessary for Christians to challenge their culture where it departs

---

8. Oden, *After Modernity*, 152.

from kingdom values; it is equally necessary for them to identify with their culture on all other matters."[9] Whether you hold a restricted view or open view of sexual and gender identity, it is not a creedal matter. Salvation does not rest in an individual's expression of sex and gender. As Christ-followers, we ought to approach this challenge in the same way we should approach any other cultural change—carefully upholding truth while passionately expressing the love of Christ.

9. Webb, *Slaves, Women and Homosexuals*, 22.

CHAPTER 4

Building a Biblical Community

Inclusion and Embrace in a Johannine View of Community

Our approach to Scripture has the power to dictate how we believe and practice the Christian faith. We must be careful not to allow our approach to restrict the movement of the Holy Spirit, or encourage us to speak against the kind of community which Christ would have us build. We all agree to this in principle, but what about in practice?

My goal is to help you love your neighbor as yourself, not to help you build higher fences. It is for this reason that the bulk of this chapter will focus on building a biblical community, rather than on the verses dealing directly with sexuality which have often been weaponized into exclusionary practices within the church. I will not be partisan to equipping well-meaning believers with verses they will use to shame and isolate the Queer community.

Too often, when we address the issues of sexuality within the church, they are done to the painful exclusion of other topics. We focus on building clever sermon series and small groups centered on issues of sex, but do they build up our community? Are our efforts pointed in the right direction to foster healthy believers and families?

Johannine Community and the Practice of Inclusion from the Fringes

"Love is a question of how one deliberately walks."[1] In this spiritually fluid generation, it is important to place focus on the community aspect of love as a means of fostering the desire for truth. Christian love can be described as actively honouring God. We best express this love through accepting God's help, power, and direction in our care for one another. If the modern Christian practices this kind of love (orthopraxy), they will naturally find themselves immersed in truth (orthodoxy) that is alive and active.

Every believer is responsible to learn and carefully apply the truth of God in the world around them through the love of Christ. All people are responsible to faithfully and lovingly act on that which they have come to know and understand. John's view of community identifies this need and incorporates it into the work of the community as a christological imperative.

The Gospel and the Epistles of John demonstrate a uniquely inclusive ideology and approach to community in Scripture. Rather than fearing what existed culturally outside the church, John upheld the truth of the Gospel "at the same time expressing it through the media of various cultures."[2] A faithful Christian community cannot be divorced from its foundations of truth and love.

While the definitive methods we should use as a church remain unspoken in John's Gospel, the later New Testament literature show us how churches began to interpret the teachings of Christ about community. Given that truth and love have been equally important parts of communal faith for believers since the Old Testament, it is not surprising that the modern church should likewise develop a pattern by which to practice this understanding. The major difficulty of this pattern for local congregations is that the role

1. Schuchard, *1–3 John*, 626.

2. Hawkin, *Johannine World*, 19.

41

of establishing and customizing it falls upon the shoulders of each pastor and congregation. This may seem daunting, but the work of creating a biblical community of inclusion and embrace is essential if we want flourishing ministries for those who are ostracized.

There are two key elements that must be retained within each plan for implementation to develop a truly Johannine ideology in a church. First, scriptural teaching must be a central component in the services and routine of the church. This means that the hearing of truth will be a visible or distinctive portion of each church gathering. Perhaps, this may mean creating a time of lection—reading God's word as a routine part of our services—or it may mean that Scripture is read from a physical Bible rather than from a smartphone. Tangible images are powerful and should be used to highlight what is necessary in the community of faith. At a personal level, engaging in devotional times is extremely important.

Secondly, we must create a distinct focus on both the inward and the outward actions of love in the community. Each person and church should strive to meet the needs both within their community of faith, and those outside of their congregation. Love is the natural response of learning truth more deeply, but it will also make the desire for knowledge of God's truth grow in a believer's heart. We must fight the urge to wait for deeper knowledge, better understanding of evangelism, or let ourselves embrace other excuses rather than allow ministries of love to emerge. God will honor those who are faithful to answer when prompted by the Holy Spirit—even if we ultimately fail.

The imbalance that is present in the modern faith community is salvageable. When a believer walks in the truth of Scripture in the way that they are called to, the apparent tension between orthodoxy and orthopraxy no longer exists. Most of us are still bearing the fruits of at least one of these two important parts of community life. Encountering the writings of John can shape the way in which we view the importance of inclusion. Truth and love represent two sides of the same goal; to experience faith means to love by living the truth in community.

A Brief Exploration of Johannine Community

John unfolds a crucial theological understanding of community in a way that draws believers into loving action. As an author, he uses distinct terminology, highlights intentional actions, and showcases specific teaching moments of Christ to help establish his view of community. Our relationships are to be founded in the truth of God and enacted with the love of God.

John 3:31–36: John Testifies about Jesus

This passage offers an in-depth look at the theological position of Christ on community. It acts as a concise reflection on the baptism of Christ (John 1:19–34) and introduces discussion of true kingdom identity and what Christian community will look like. The community of faith will remain founded on the eternal God, but will be shaped by the incarnate Christ and evidenced by the presence of the Holy Spirit.

John 4:7–15, 31–34: Jesus Widens Community to Include the Excluded

The reason that compelled Christ to travel through Samaria is not given; Scripture is clear that Jesus' travel route was not the normative path. However, it is clear that the decisions of Christ are consistently rooted in the will of the Father. This does not only show the dedication of Jesus to the will of the Father, but also shows the nature of Christian community which is rooted in "true worship being the worship of the Father in spirit and truth" through acts of love and obedience.[3]

As an isolated incident, John 4:1–44 appears to be more focused on the Messianic teachings and the reuniting of Samaria and Judea. However, in the wider context of the Gospel of John, there is evidence that Christ was acting out of the imperative to create holistic community. "On two accounts Jesus should not speak to

3. Maloney, *Gospel of John*, 139.

her: she is a woman, and she is a Samaritan . . . yet Jesus opens the discussion with an imperative: 'give me a drink.'"[4] Christ engages her in a community that reaches beyond that which is culturally appropriate for the purpose of creating a new normal.

This account calls into question the Jewish ritual purity as Jesus shares a cup with a woman who was from a "bastardized" former part of Israel known as Samaria.[5] This would have been considered a "seriously polluting act by Pharisee standards," especially given the privacy of the conversation.[6] The new standards for community are to go beyond the expectations of humanity by engaging the *spirit of the law* rather than the *letter of the law.*

The use of food and water as illustrations in this narrative also act as primary witnesses to the new standards of community. Christ not only reorients the understanding of the woman who stands in sin outside the community, but also the men who dwell within the inner circle. Christ gives the Samaritan woman an unexpected and unprecedented invitation to participate in community through his description and offering of "living water" (John 4:10). Christ, likewise, reshapes the image of community in conversation with the disciples by the initial refusal of physical food, followed by the description of food as doing "the will of him who sent me and to complete his work" (John 4:34).

The Samaritan woman also sees the distance that should exist between herself, as a disgraced female Samaritan, and Jesus, as a holy Jewish man. "The woman's response highlights the irregularity of the encounter. It has a nuance of mockery."[7] Her response, which falls in line with the common worldview of the Samaritans, was laced with insulting tones aimed in the direction of the Jewish man with whom she was speaking.[8] Christ's offer of inclusion was so unexpected, she mistook it for further insults and responded in kind.

---

4. Maloney, *Gospel of John*, 117.

5. Malina and Rohrbaugh, *Social-Science Commentary*, 98.

6. Malina and Rohrbaugh, *Social-Science Commentary*, 99.

7. Maloney, *Gospel of John*, 117.

8. Maloney, *Gospel of John*, 117.

The conversation is not only striking for the fact that it overlooks the current cultural position of the Samaritan woman, but that it transforms her cultural position. Through the discussion that takes place in the narrative of John 4, the Samaritan woman is interpersonally transformed, and no longer remains a person with whom it is culturally inappropriate to engage in conversation.[9] Christ's interaction is not only countercultural but is deeply transformational for those who are involved. "The promise of Jesus transcends this person, this place, this water, this well, and this time."[10]

John 5:34–47: Further Testimonies about Jesus

Following the healing of a man "who had been ill for 38 years" (John 5:3), and the murderous intent that Christ's actions evoked in hearts of the Jewish leadership (John 5:18), Jesus examines what it means to live in community. This placement is important to note because Christ takes this healing and response of anger as an opportunity to identify who belongs in the conversation.

By using broadly inclusive language, Jesus not only addresses those who were angry, but all Jews present for the discourse. Christ responds by explaining the divine origin of authority as the basis for his choice to heal. In identifying the authority of the Son of God and the community to which this message was given, we can determine Christ's ideal image of community as presented in John's Gospel. "The authorities' unwillingness to acknowledge Jesus' claims calls into question their commitment to Scripture, the very heart of their faith, and basis of their hope of life."[11] Ultimately, Christ is proclaiming that their belief in God requires their faithful and loving actions in the community.

9. Malina and Rohrbaugh, *Social-Science Commentary*, 99.

10. Maloney, *Gospel of John*, 118.

11. Michaels, *Gospel of John*, 97.

John 13:1–17:26: Conversations in the Upper Room

In this passage, Jesus employs a practice that was common in ancient Hellenistic festive meals known as a "symposium."[12] This practice was the conclusion of festivities that began with a meal and ritual washings. The concluding symposium discussion was initiated and directed by the guest of honor. Christ is not only intentional in the action of washing the disciples's feet, but in the manner in which the discussion is timed. Jesus intentionally triggers an early symposium during this meal. This act is countercultural, but as such, serves to spark focused conversation that goes beyond the surface level of faithful understanding and practice.

This symposium meal, which begins in John 13:1, is interrupted by the uncomfortable confrontation between Jesus and Judas. This conversation follows the foot-washing act and results in Judas's departure from the upper room (John 13:30). Despite the palpable tensions which surrounded the symposium, Christ continued to teach the disciples.[13]

This is a critical moment in which Christ embodies the principles that drive the ideology of the Gospel of John most clearly. Christ shows immense love through service, and uses this as a moment in which to inspire and remind the disciples of their relationship with the Father. This depiction of love—considering the teachings that follow—will set the tone for the interrelation of the Godhead and the Christian community that emerges in the first and second centuries.

The love that is expressed in this passage through the act of foot-washing cannot be divorced from the concept of obedience to truth. As a result of this controversial act of love, Jesus begins a time of teaching. This teaching continues throughout this passage, and into the chapters that follow, showing the connection between the examples of love and the explicit commands that are given by Christ.

---

12. Malina and Rohrbaugh, *Social-Science Commentary*, 227.

13. These tensions are evident in both Christ becoming "troubled in spirit" (John 13:21) and in the uncertainty of the disciples (John 13:22). This is also present in the immediacy of Judas's departure from the meal they were sharing (John 13:30).

The disciples that Christ chose also highlight the kind of love that is offered by God to humanity. Jesus loves the disciples, even those who will fail as was predicted of them. This steadfast and unchanging love acts as "the final proof for his claim to be the one who makes God known."[14]

In line with the pollution of engaging in conversation with the Samaritan woman, Christ lowers his own standing within the Jewish community for the purpose of creating a new vision of community. The love of Christ in this passage is described as crossing "all boundaries of living: he loves his disciples consummately."[15] Love, as presented in this section, is rooted in the understanding of the final words of John 13:1, εἰς τέλος (*eis telos*—meaning *to the end*). This discussion branches from the introduction to Christ's act of love in the foot-washing encounter: "Now before the festival of the Passover, Jesus knew that his hour had come to depart from this world and go to the Father. Having loved his own who were in the world, *he loved them to the end*" (John 13:1, emphasis added). This love is deep and reflects the deeply connected and committed love that is found within the confines of a permanent relationship—such as a marriage.

The concept of love within this passage explains the communal act of showing love, and acts as "John's term for loyalty and group attachment."[16] In light of εἰς τέλος, this love is not only community-centric, but also a permanent binding to Christ and the kingdom of God. The love of Jesus and his followers requires mutual, all-encompassing, everlasting commitment.[17]

The act of foot washing that takes place is a primary depiction of Christ's love through intentional actions. In this act, the reader is

14. Maloney, *Gospel of John*, 116.

15. Maloney, *Gospel of John*, 105.

16. Malina and Rohrbaugh, *Social-Science Commentary*, 218.

17. Malina and Rohrbaugh use this discussion to show the communal aspects of the relationship between Christ and the disciples. They also touch on the importance of this discussion in light of the impending conversation about Christ's departure. Here, to speak tritely, Christ establishes the longevity of the relationship so that when the time of his departure comes, the movement which has been created will continue on.

forced to consider not only the action of washing feet, but also the motivation behind a degrading act that was reserved for servants or slaves.[18] Thus, the reader is confronted by John's "move from the ordinary use of language and behavior relating to foot washing to the antilanguage and symbolic behavior of the Johannine antisociety."[19]

In this act, the normative understanding of the roots of love are changed. Christ shows a love that has personal costs—defying the norm which elevated "self-love [as] the standard."[20] In Old Testament law, and even within that which is found elsewhere in the New Testament, the reasoning for loving others is often contingent upon the love of one's self.[21] The Johannine counterculture is one that is not merely rooted in a doctrinal or societal variance, nor is it meant to create an alternative society in which Christians can dwell.

"Christian community is not an end in itself," but is rather intended to create a culture from which we can minister and invite others to experience the dramatic gospel of love.[22] It is through this intentionally countercultural and counterintuitive action that Jesus is able to establish the truth that must guide the Johannine community of faith. Peter's confrontation introduces the arc of teaching that will define the next four chapters of the Gospel.

As a chapter, John 14 fits well within the established rhythm of this teaching and demonstration by Christ. It is in this chapter, however, that the description of communion with Christ is initially

---

18. Malina and Rohrbaugh, *Social-Science Commentary*, 220.

19. Malina and Rohrbaugh, *Social-Science Commentary*, 220.

20. Koester, *Word of Life*, 194.

21. In the NRSV, the verses that indicate love of self as the rationale of love for others include:
Lev 19:18—"You shall love your neighbor *as yourself*."
Matt 22:39—"You shall love your neighbor *as yourself*."
Mark 12:31—"You shall love your neighbor *as yourself*."
Luke 10:27—"You shall love the Lord your God with all your heart, and with all your soul, and with all your strength, and with all your mind; and your neighbor *as yourself*."
Rom 13:9—"Love your neighbor *as yourself*."
Gal 5:14—"You shall love your neighbor *as yourself*."
Jas 2:8—"You shall love your neighbor *as yourself*."

22. Koester, *Word of Life*, 195.

given in the most concise manner. John 14:15 presents a contingency between the actions of abiding by God's truth, and the act of loving God.

The commandments found in the Gospel of John are important not only for the directives within them, but rather for the simple fact that they exist. Of the New Testament Gospels, John gives "remarkably few specific commands about what to do or not do. There is no list of virtues and vices, no detailed manual on how to act in each situation."[23] This stands apart from that which is found in other gospels, such as the Sermon on the Mount in Matt 5–7 which provides set standards of conduct for specific communal engagements.

John's Gospel is less concerned with the minor details of God's commands, but rather chooses to include the metanarrative view. For this reason, "when Jesus does give a command he makes comprehensive claims in very few words."[24] The claims are infrequent, but when they are visible within the text of the Gospel, they are concise and impact several areas of the believer's life.

Viewing love in the context of a commandment may be difficult for modern readers of the Gospel to fathom. However, the original audience may have had a more inclusive view of the two concepts. While love can still include a sense of "intimacy and depth of feeling . . . it is primarily a bond of commitment."[25] God's command in the Gospel of John was not merely a command to affection, but was rather a command to remain faithful to him in the same way that each spouse has expectations of faithfulness for their partner.

The command to love, as witnessed in John 14, is a prime example of John's concise approach to commands. In John's Gospel, Christ says, "If you love me, you will keep my commandments . . . Whoever does not love me does not keep my words; and the word that you hear is not mine, but is from the Father who sent me" (John 14:15, 24). In these two appearances of God's commandments in

23. Koester, *Word of Life*, 188.

24. Koester, *Word of Life*, 188.

25. Koester, *Word of Life*, 190.

the Gospel of John, there is succinct language that is open to a wide array of spiritual applications.

This may appear less informative—and formative—than the commands which are found in the synoptics or other New Testament literature.[26] However, there is power in the instructions that are given through these concise words. This power is reflective of the one who calls for obedience, but also the empowerment of those who are to discern the means of obedience.

This power is also contingent upon the love of the believer for the one to whom they are showing obedience. If a person has love for the one to whom they are obedient, and their obedience is contingent upon such, their dedication to love others will presumably increase. John's lack of specific commandments for obedience, is not an oversight, but rather the *empowerment* of believers to show their love for Christ. Truth requires love to enable the believer to engage in authentic worship of God, rather than mere adherence to a legal code.

It is interesting that this command is first presented positively, and then later presented within the chapter negatively. This appears to be reflective in terminology, but also in terms of the structural format of the passage. In order to strengthen the argument and remind the audience of the importance of this command, it is given both positively and negatively. This command also saturates the language of John 15 and becomes a central focus of discussion.

Rooted within the concept that is presented in John's Gospel, there is little room for divorcing right understanding from right practice. In this ideology, the knowledge of God's commands anticipates faithfulness to God's will as a means of showing love. Love is thus marked by obedience. Similarly, obedience depends on the knowledge of truth. For the Gospel writer, these are not individual concepts, but rather a single entity—truth and love witnessed in

---

26. This difference is most evident in the way that the commands are taught in the beatitudes of Matt 5–7 as opposed to this expression. While it takes more than these two chapters to express what it means to be in Christian community in the Gospel of Matthew, John expresses this concept within the content in a single verse. This is likewise true of the other Gospels.

obedience is a sign that we are becoming a community with God and others.

While each of these specific moments of teaching are foundational to this discussion, John's view of Christian community is vividly depicted in the teaching moments of John 15:1–17. This section views love as a command by itself, however, in the context of the larger Gospel of John, this command cannot be reduced to affection, but must also include obedience. To show the love of God to one another is to remain obedient to God's truth and commandments. Abiding in God means that a person is not only listening to, but obeying the will of God—causing them to be bearers of fruit.[27]

This is the expectation that is placed upon those who are connected to the vine—we are expected to bear fruit in our lives. "I am the true vine, and my Father is the vinegrower. He removes every branch in me that *bears no fruit*. Every branch that bears fruit he prunes to make it *bear more fruit*" (John 15:1–2, italics added). The expectation of Christian community in the Gospel of John is clearly tied to how a person shows their commitment to their faith.

This passage explains the source of the love and the reason for such obedience to truth is necessary. Jesus is identified as a channel through which the love of God can flow to believers. This relationship between the Father and the Son hinges not on divinity, but rather upon obedience and love. Likewise, "the disciples are to repeat . . . what Jesus has always had with the Father: a loving mutuality shown by the unconditional observance of his commandments."[28] Not only does the bond between Christ and the Father show the source from which love can emerge, but it also provides an example of fruit-bearing.[29]

This text is not only focused upon the actions of the believer and what fruit is produced in their lives, but also upon the means in which that is formed. In this way, the passage sets the tone for what discipleship in Christian community should look like. Fruit is produced through showing others the same love that Christ has

27. Koester, *Word of Life*, 195.

28. Maloney, *Gospel of John*, 422.

29. Koester, *Word of Life*, 196.

shown to the believer, but it must be rooted in the message which Christ brings. "By giving love and keeping Jesus' word, faith comes to fruition."[30]

In this simple prayer spoken by Christ in John 17:25-26, there is a deep-rooted theology of integration between the knowledge of God and the expression of divine love.[31] This prayer shows the intrinsic union of truth and love in the community of the believer with God and with one another. Christ's relationship with the Father is dependent on knowledge and is enacted through love.

In the earlier verses of this chapter, Jesus' prayer focuses on a desire for the disciples to engage in the mission of God. "Jesus has come to the moment of his final self-gift in love . . . [as a means of showing them a godly desire for a community] . . . made holy in the truth."[32] This prayerful imagery of truth is an indication of Christ's emphatic hope for their future community.

The importance of this prayer, theologically, is witnessed most clearly in the pinnacle verses of 17:25-26. In this final section of the prayer, Jesus unifies the knowledge of God the Father with the love of God, and others. In making God known to the disciples, Christ shows the "love that bonds the Father and the Son [so that it] might bond the disciples, [and] that they might be loved by God in the same way that the Father has loved the Son."[33]

A Christian community, in the Johannine worldview, is marked by the pursuit of holiness through the truth and love. John's ultimate goal, in the perspective of Francis J. Maloney, is to see disciples be made holy through their knowledge of God intertwined with their experience of the love of God and each other.[34] Truth and love must be equally embraced within God's holy kingdom.

---

30. Koester, *Word of Life*, 196.

31. "Righteous Father, the world does not know you, but I know you; and these know that you have sent me. I made your name known to them, and I will make it known, so that the love with which you have loved me may be in them, and I in them" (John 17:25-26).

32. Maloney, *Gospel of John*, 469.

33. Maloney, *Gospel of John*, 476.

34. Maloney, *Gospel of John*, 477.

The Radical Nature of Johannine Community

While John explains that the truth should lead to the expression of love, he has also given comments about the importance of safeguarding the community. "Some commentators brand John's teaching un-Christian," but it is important to note who the recipients of such critical exclusion were.[35] It was not the poor, widows, or orphans of whom John was speaking, rather exclusion was reserved for those who could and would bring destruction into the community *willfully*.

As someone who already knew the teachings of God, the sins of the Samaritan woman were dangerous when left unmentioned or unaddressed. Christ and her local community knew that she was a woman who had already expended five husbands and was currently participating in a relationship that was not a valid matrimonial arrangement (John 4:18). The pride of the disciples in the John 13 narrative was equally as dangerous to the community. In both situations, Christ called for a measure of repentance in order to safeguard the community (John 4:16–28; 13:8–11).

Theologically and narratively speaking, it is common in Johannine literature to see this method of imparting ideological standards to the community. In 2 John, a similar occurrence exists following the impartation of the discussion of God's command. 2 John 7–11 give a similar, yet drastic warning against participation in activities which can taint the community.

In John's perspective, Christ was clearly intended to be the center of community values, and practices. To intermingle with people who did not share similar values at a *spiritual* level was akin to adopting their values. This distance is not defined by cultural standards, but rather is decided by the standards of Christ's ideology of community. John's distance is a definitive rejection of allowing false teachers in the community.

John's strong language is not the only aspect of his argument which explains the seriousness of his position on protecting the community. The nature of this command, in and of itself, denotes the importance which he places on this discussion. Hospitality, as a

35. Schuchard, *1–3 John*, 633.

practice in the world of the New Testament, "was not only a social necessity, but also established or reinforced bonds between different communities."[36]

All were welcomed freely to belong to the community of faith, and to understand God's role in creation and our lives. However, John's view of community wraps loving community in the protective shield of truth that is meant to give a firm christological foundation. Once you come to know the truth of Scripture, you are made accountable to uphold that truth—just as we are accountable to the call to love one another.

Johannine Community in Scriptural Comparison

John approaches his depiction of the life of the believer in the same way that each book of the Holy Scriptures does: using a motif or theme. John's presentation of the christological narrative does this considering the view of community. In the context of the rest of Scripture, John's ideology does not cause disagreement or fragmentation of the larger message of Christ. While the implementation of this community is uniquely Johannine, the goals remain consistent with the larger presentation of the Holy Scriptures. These goals are particularly aligned with the goals and desires of the Jewish tradition.

The message of the Gospel of John is "profoundly social in character," despite the fact that Johannine literature as a whole presents an alternative or anti-society.[37] The social character of this gospel is not only concerned with the exclusivity of a particular ideology and theology, but is dedicated to broad inclusion. In this way, the ideology of John is reflective of Paul's perspective of community inclusion and exclusion.

While the broadly inclusive view of John's community is also witnessed elsewhere in the New Testament, Gal 3:28 and Eph 5:1–20 are the most directly linked passages in terms of a practical ideology. While the Samaritans, mentioned in John's Gospel,

36. Lieu, *Theology of the Johannine Epistles*, 261.

37. Malina and Rohrbaugh, *Social-Science Commentary*, 19.

originated from the Jews, the southern kingdom of Israel did not regard them as continued heirs to the promise of God. Both John and Paul overturn this perception in the narrative accounts and the directives that reflect the actions of Jesus. In Galatians 3:28, Paul's broadly inclusive call to Christian community is reminiscent of Christ's offer of "living water" (John 4:11) to the Samaritan woman and her community (John 4:1–42).

Paul's works are also reflective of the John's perspective in their attention to both truth and love. Eph 5:1–20 calls believers to imitate Christ in both their actions and their understanding of all that is "good and right and true" (Eph 5:9). In this call to action, Paul also places a firm emphasis on the fact that orthodoxy stems from finding out "what is pleasing to the Lord" (Eph 5:10) and acting in that truth.

PART TWO

Avoiding Ministries That Kill Community

CHAPTER 5

Things to Avoid in Practical Church Ministry

Identifying Community-Killers in the Church

As we begin to address our own ministries and practices, we must first pull the weeds from our gardens. In likeness to growing fruit and vegetables, you cannot grow healthy ministries when there are weeds waiting to choke them out. With youth pastors in the Wesleyan Church reporting as many as 60 percent of their teens expressing experimentation with and embrace of alternative sexual and gender identities, we must pay closer attention to what we do and say as the church.[1] Should we fail to address—and remove—weed-like ministries in our churches, our attempts to empower Christlikeness will run the enormous risk of harming our communities.

---

1. As reported in private interviews with a large selection of youth pastors from the Wesleyan Church equally distributed in rural, suburban, and urban settings of the USA and Canada.

Targeted Queer Ministries

Common Example: 12-Step Ministries

Why this kills community: This creates a divide between Queer individuals seeking Christ from the rest of the body of Christ.

When there is a problem in the community, our first thought is often to create a program, small group, or life group to solve it. This is the most common misstep that we can make as pastors and leaders. Rather than offering blanket solutions, we must look to the individual needs we can meet and understand the social atmosphere that is created by the types of helps we offer.

Those in conservative churches must be especially careful not to treat the members of our congregations who are also members of the Queer community in the same way you might help those struggling with an addiction. While members within the community—just like anyone else—may struggle with addictive aspects of their lives, we must not approach sexual or gender identity in the same way as alcoholism. Using Celebrate Recovery (or other 12-step programs) as a form of conversion therapy is little more than an act of *codependent behavior* by leadership.

It is understandable that not all Christians interpret Scripture the same way, and that some have concluded that sexual and gender identities other than binary, heterosexual cisgender is acceptable. It is beyond rational comprehension to view—and treat others—as though their identity beyond this limited scope is on the same level as the disease of addictions. Why do we keep offering 12-step programs geared at changing everything about these precious members of God's kingdom?

There are a host of reasons why we should move away from this type of misdirected ministry as the solution for navigating questions of sexual and gender identity/expression. The primary issue is that it will almost certainly drive people away from Christ. In directly confronting an already sensitive and vulnerable area of an individual's life without personalized care and concern, we will almost certainly end up hurting people. When a person comes to the community of faith and is seeking to a place to belong, why would we think it is acceptable to put conditions on their journey towards Christ?

Twelve-step programs such as Celebrate Recovery are conditional by nature—requiring ongoing specific changes in an individual's life. While these programs work wonderfully for certain areas of ministry, they are not appropriate or designed to be used for all situations and circumstances. If we maintain these types of ministries for the purpose of a broad spectrum of lifestyle alteration, we tarnish their effectiveness in the targeted areas of ministry for which they are designed to be used.

Shame has never been a responsible or effective tool to encourage spiritual growth. Sexual identity is often fused to the identity of an individual. When conservative churches try to help people find sexual transformation rather than fleshing out their identity in Christ, they take away the beauty of their souls rather than enabling them to welcome the Holy Spirit and the life they seek. In practicing this kind of disillusioned ministry, we are not transforming the world for the kingdom of God, we are crusading against it.

Utilizing recovery ministries to navigate sexual and gender identity kills community because they were never designed to help in situations of sexual and gender identity. Rather than breathing life and the love of God as they do in situations of addictions, misusing these programs only pours shame into vulnerable hearts. If this is the only ministry that your church offers to the Queer community, it would be better if you did not offer anything. There has already been enough perceived shame and condemnation from the church.

Sin Removal over Spiritual Growth

Common Example: Pray-the-Gay-Out Support Groups

Why this kills community: This type of ministry creates a deep-rooted sense of shame instead of a desire for spiritual growth. It often results in disappointment and the emergence of failure culture.

As a fifteenth-century minister, Martin Luther is best known for writing the Ninety-Five Theses of the church and causing the divide within the Catholic Church that would ultimately lead to the creation of the Protestant church. This important reformer was also responsible for the propagation of a less-than-ideal ministry model—*sin removal leads to spiritual growth*. While theologically this idea may hold some sense of truth, there is danger in practicing this vision of the faith.

In practice, when our ministries focus on the removal of sin—rather than spiritual growth—they often end in disaster. Think of this choice in terms of areas of our life: you would not consciously spend all your time gardening focused on killing the weeds. While weed removal is good, it is important that you also look to the needs of what you are trying to grow. If all you do is pull weeds out, and never plant your vegetable seeds or care for them, all you are accomplishing is the first step in creating a spiritual desert.

For churches that believe in limited gender and sexual identity, an extra measure of care must be given in ministry. While the aim is for personal holiness in sexual identity, ministry can often descend into "pray the gay out" retreats or sin removal if the approach is from the angle taught and expressed in practice by Martin Luther. This is true of any issue, but especially true for those who struggle with their understanding of personal identity.

When we use ministries that focus on sin removal, we create a spiritual vacuum. This may work short term, but there are severe long-term consequences to these types of ministries. It is often out of these ministries that people realize that the aspects of their lives they removed were important to them, and begin to regret the choices they made. When spiritual emphasis is misplaced in our ministries, we leave people ill-equipped to truly deal with sin in their lives.

When people are ill-equipped to deal with sin and have little to no foundation on which to build their faith, they tend to fail more frequently in their attempts to overcome sin. This creates a failure culture—a two-pronged problem of defeat and deity. Spiritual defeat creates a belief that either we are not strong enough or faithful enough to overcome sin, or that God is not good enough to help.

Individuals seeking spiritual help may expect permanent cures that *we* cannot offer. In this failure culture, the experience of non-hetero attraction or non-binary identification reflects on God's inability or vindictiveness more than human struggles with sin. Ultimately, whether it happens in ten days or ten years, the person who is ill-equipped will recognize that they cannot win in their struggle with sin.

Many who realize their consistently losing battle will walk away from the faith rooted in the belief that either their sexual practice is not sinful or that they are too broken for God to help. Faithful believers feeling the weight of failure cultures such as this often develop a mantra of thinking, "*If it was sinful, why won't God help me overcome it?*" As a result of our own poor teaching and equipping, these individuals can become militantly opposed to the future help of the church. Why should we expect them to trust a community that only brought more pain, more shame, and more hardship into their lives?

These types of ministries are also dangerous from a legal standpoint—especially for Canadian churches. Given that the goal is sin removal and not the enriching of a person's life, they easily cross the line into what is considered conversion therapy. This practice has been criminalized in Canada due to the incredibly destructive pattern it creates. Conversion therapy elevates the risk of suicide attempts by 75 percent and attempts resulting in permanent injury or ongoing health effects by 88 percent.[2]

Before we cry foul over this intervention of government in church practice, let us also take note that over 80 percent of these individuals at elevated risk for suicide experienced their sexual orientation change experiences or conversion therapy in the churches they attended.[3] We, as pastors and Christians, have been the *direct cause* of attempted suicides.

Emily was a young woman who had attended church events for most of her life. In high school she, as many others do, began to explore her sexual identity. Through her journey, she realized that

2. Blosnich et al., *Sexual Orientation*, 1024–30.
3. Blosnich et al., *Sexual Orientation*, 1024–30.

she had an attraction to women. During this journey of self-discovery, she also began attending a local church with her best friend. She felt that she had found a community that genuinely supported and loved her.

The faith community did care for her deeply and they recognized her struggle to discern her identity. Eventually, the pastoral team decided that the next step in her faith journey would be to undergo conversion therapy. With little say in her own personal journey, she was told that she was "wrong, and full of evil."[4] All the things that she had just discovered and formed her identity out of needed to change for her to continue to be a part of the community she loved.

She now struggles with the ongoing damage from that conversion therapy—including the aftermath of several failed suicide attempts. Her mental and physical health consequences will permanently require ongoing medical care. As a result of her trauma in conversion therapy, she does not currently attend a church and suffered the rejection of a community that she loved deeply. She loves God, but now hopes to worship in a faith community that will not treat her with that kind of love that leaves her with bruises and battle scars.

Why does the government and medical community need to tell us something about ministry that Scripture already tells us? Sin removal is the practice of living under the law. When our focus shifts to spiritual growth, it is easier to recognize that risking the health and welfare of one of God's children does not bring him glory.

---

4. Quote from private interview.

Controversial Partnerships (Political and Social)

Common Example: Affiliations to Christian Organizations or Politicians

Why this kills community: Regardless of our position statements as churches and denominations, partnering with groups inconsistent with our own ideals can create disastrous divides in our local community and presents an unwelcoming atmosphere that may not actually exist.

We live in a culture where most people will not go out to a restaurant or gym without looking up a recommendation or review on the place. Why do we expect that people would treat church any differently? What will our references and affiliations communicate to others during their web search?

This does not mean that you should hide the ministries you support on your websites and then continue supporting organizations with questionable practices towards the Queer community. Trust me, no amount of stealth will hide things that you do not want to be found. Ask any politician that has even a hint of a questionable choice in their past.

John and Sarah were invited to attend a dinner with another family in their church. They were excited about this meal, as they were told that they would also have the chance to hear a special speaker of high renown. The couple felt that it would be a good opportunity to go and get to know the local church members who had invited them and they decided to accept their invitation.

Upon arriving, John and Sarah quickly realized that the special dinner was a political rally from a frighteningly far-right American political group known for their anti-gay and pro-life platforms. By the end of the night, John felt so uncomfortable that he even expressed to Sarah that he feared his immigration status would be rejected by their attendance of a rally such as this—even though he and Sarah were both pro-life and believed in monogamous heterosexual marriage.

When John shared this story privately with the senior pastor, the pastor admitted that he had also attended one of these extremely uncomfortable dinners in a previous year and decided it was not a good look to be affiliated with them. However, at the next annual church meeting, under the budget line item of community giving, John realized that the name of the questionable group was included. This inconsistency did not sit well with the couple; John and Sarah left the church within six months.

While politically this is more prevalent in the more conservative areas within United States and Canada, social partnerships (including those with questionable Christian organizations) can have grave consequences for ministry. I trust that we would never do something as ignorant and inappropriate as minister in *blackface*. Are we ignorantly choosing to support those who harm others by using the gospel like a weapon against members of the Queer community? If we truly desire to create a community in which all people feel welcomed to come and experience God's grace and transformation, we must not put barricades in front of the door.

We must be careful not to tie a millstone around the neck of our spiritual children as we minister to them. Be certain to investigate the beliefs and practices of each group you support. Look into more than what they advertise they support or disagree with; ask the questions about *how* they minister. Is their view of outreach to the Queer community protesting or street-preaching about the evils of their identity or do they offer the love of Christ in a tangible way?

There are also controversial partnerships that exist within the walls of our churches that teach non-heteronormative, cisgender, or gender binary families/individuals that they are not welcomed into the community. These ministry partnerships can include:

- **Singles Ministry and Marriage Ministry:** While singles/celibacy ministries are actually positive for the LGBTQ+ community, singles ministry often devolves into a single-and-ready-to-mingle ministry which ultimately focuses on pairing singles off or preparing them for marriage. This kind of culture paired with a singles ministry naturally creates a barrier for asexual individuals especially.

- **Marriage and Family Ministries:** The interconnection of these two ministries is a barrier to families that will come to your church that do not fit the heteronormative spectrum. Imagine how isolating it would be if you found an incredible place where your kids are growing and changing, but then you find yourself and your partner naturally excluded because they only ever talk about hetero partnership needs and, within their children's programs, idolize the image of a perfect happy heteronormative family. While it can be healthy to interconnect marriages and family ministries for those in heteronormative partnerships, it lessens the importance of anyone who does not fit that mold. A single mom may find a great place for her kids to grow in your church, but then experience the deep sense of loneliness that comes from exclusion—by proxy of event focus or by the experiences of her children on an extravagantly celebrated Father's Day.

- **Marriage-Heavy Language/Emphasis:** When our ministries—regardless of their focus—have a heavy focus on the importance of marriage, or emphasize marriage in our language, we partner the church with the "1950s Disney" philosophy that we are not made complete until we, as cisgender individuals, are partnered with our perfect heterosexual cisgender spouse. Ultimately, this limits the space for individuals who are not in heteronormative partnerships or identify as cisgender in the kingdom of God.

What kind of faith do we want our churches to communicate? When we allow these kinds of community-killers to infest the ministries of our churches, the consequence is that we harm those to whom we seek to minister. Rather than expressing the love of God, they teach people that church is hate-filled and only for those who meet the terms and conditions we arbitrarily decide upon.

CHAPTER 6

Things to Avoid as Individuals Ministering to Our Communities

Identifying Community-Killers in Individual Ministry Situations

"We love your church, and your ministries are really great
for our kids, but there is a person in your church that has
consistently said and done things to hurt us as a family. We
won't be coming back after today."

Our churches may have a much larger voice, but the voice of a single
person can speak to what the community *truly* believes and practices. We had just finished a service in which the Spirit was moving
and people were making commitments that would transform their
lives. Our kids ministry was about to launch a new and exciting
season, our youth group was growing, and a few of our other ministries had also recently exploded in growth. It was then that the
words in the quote above were spoken to us about one member
of our community for what would neither be the first nor the last

time. Community-killers can also exist within the individual role and choices of the Christian, leader, or pastor.

Public Forum Condemnation

Common Example: Preaching or Protesting

Why this kills community: This creates a holy hierarchy of sins which falsely represents the gospel and the intentions of Scripture.

Have you ever sat in a meeting at work when you know that other team members have also failed to meet their objectives, but the only one that is called out is you? You may not have even realized that there was a problem, but the longer they criticize you publicly, the more you may feel a sense of disconnect with your boss. Perhaps you even want to quit and work for someone who recognizes your worth as a team member despite your faults.

When we talk about issues of sexual identity or sexual practices in isolation, the same sense of disconnect can happen between you and those who are living that reality. We already recognize and treat other subjects with greater care, but when it comes to sexual and gender identity, the tendency for conservative Christians can be to think that preaching fire and brimstone is the only way. It may be all too easy to rise to the pulpit and spend our entire sermon on the evils of sexual or gender divergence without ever addressing the heterosexual premarital sex elephant sitting in the third, seventh, and ninth rows. When addressing sensitive issues, we cannot address them in isolation or without compassion.

For those who do not support all forms of identity, there is danger in talking about sexual issues from the pulpit. This caution also applies to other public forum and platforms—like social media. I would encourage you to strongly consider finding other forums that remove pressure from the subject and allow for more open dialogue. Consider how easy it is for someone to misinterpret what you say, and how easy it is for others to access apps like Twitter in the midst of that misunderstanding. You could easily become the avatar of straight pride with one screenshot or under-informed tweet. Sensitive conversations deserve a safe space for open dialogue—public forums do not allow for this kind of care.

When Jeremy was forcefully outed to his church, most of the congregation immediately unfriended him on social media. He had already had a tremendously long struggle with his sexual identity. He had tried to reconcile his personal identity with his faith, including a desperate attempt at conversion therapy, followed by his equally desperate attempt at suicide.

Knowing he could not continue without support and care, Jeremy prayed and asked God for wisdom. He begged that God would reveal to him whether he should keep trying to practice faith in the same congregation that had emotionally abused him. He faithfully laid a fleece out before God and told God that if homosexuality or sexual identity were to be mentioned—even in passing—that would be God's confirmation to find a new church family. "Lo, and behold, that was the topic of that evening's sermon. I haven't been back."[1] Jeremy loves Jesus; he also needs to feel safe to worship in community.

For those who are not in a position of preaching, it is still our responsibility to also guard the types of public forums you use to talk about gender and sexual identity. In Toronto, there is a large intersection near the Eaton Centre where Young and Dundas Streets meet. For those who may be unfamiliar with it, the area is like a Canadian version of Times Square. It also happens to be located just south of the famed church and Wellesley Gay Pride District.

At any time of any day of any week, you can go to this intersection and find people loudly talking about the evils of homosexuality and protesting Queer rights. Well-meaning individuals will stand and decry the evils of sexual sins—missing the plank in their own eyes as they are arrested for assault when the sin of their anger boils over at someone hurt by their message. During 2018, the only times that we saw Christians in the news or our Twitter feeds mentioning Toronto was when they were rightly arrested for physically attacking others—typically due to this type of ill-practice in ministry.

---

1. Quote from private interview.

Pamphlet and Track Methodology

Common Example: Rainbow Tracts

Why this kills community: Tracts do not allow the space to deal with the complexity of this issue and leave people confused and angered by insufficient or inflammatory messaging.

We sat down to play a game with new friends at a gaming store and one of our new friends perked up saying that he found something hilarious and deeply shameful at a store the day previous. What he pulled out of his bag made David and I blanch—after all, these new friends we had only met a week or so before had no idea that we were Christians, let alone ordained ministers. What our new friend revealed to us was a tract talking about the evils of playing Dungeons and Dragons.

It seems laughable now, given that this was the very type of game we were about to play. Yet, the damage of the ill-informed tract was done. While we did gain the opportunity to talk to each of our new friends about our faith and work as pastors in the community, the bad taste of that tract never left their mouths. Printed words can never be unprinted.

The real problem that arises with utilizing a tract that broaches issues of sexual identity is that they do not allow for questions and conversation. When approaching delicate subjects such as sexual and gender identity, we must not close the door to conversations and questions. Tracts are also dangerous as they often present a version of the sin removal over spiritual growth pattern that can affect our church ministries negatively.

One proud pastor recently showed me a rainbow flag tract he created for the purpose of handing out in June during Pride month—perhaps even at a Pride parade. He felt that this pamphlet would genuinely lead to the salvation of many who came into possession of the tract. Tracts such as this are generally written by those with little to no factual knowledge about life in LGBTQIA2S+ communities and the hardships they face as individuals. This leader had

71

all the right intentions, but no understanding of or sensitivity to the needs of his local Queer community.

Faith is not an excuse for ignorance, but that is the message that tracts tend to communicate when they are overly targeted and under-informed. Tracts of this nature can have the potential to ruin ministries when a hurt person deems that your message of perceived hate is viral-worthy. They can ruin your image in a matter of minutes and leave a mess that will take years to address—if it can ever be corrected.

A non-denominational church in eastern Canada used inflammatory messaging and was swarmed by social media. Despite several attempts at rebranding the church, including five location changes and four names—ten years later, the church is still known as the group that were ignorant and hateful to others. Their pastors and members have even lost their apartments/homes, and secular jobs because of their affiliation with this church that is perceived as a hate group. Some members of the leadership team were even in considerable danger of actionable charges being pressed against them—resulting in potential jail time for their hate crimes.

Assumptions of Understanding (Psychology Culture)

Common Example: Assumptions of Reasons for Sexual Identity

Why this kills community: We appear (and are) ignorant to an individual's story and identity making a further hurdle or obstacle between Christ and those we are trying to reach out to.

When I was a young teen, I was told by several trusted leaders in several churches that lesbians choose to love women because they have been abused by a male and therefore are more likely to trust women with intimacy. This idea might seem reasonable enough until someone you know expresses a same-sex attraction and you are confronted with your perception of truth. While it may be true that abuse can contribute to a transition of sexuality, this is not always the experience of an individual. Overgeneralization is a dangerous practice that has become commonplace when it comes our perceptions of identity.

One of the biggest assumptions that some Christians have made within the church is that sexual and gender identity are always a sinful and willful choice. This may feel like a very bold statement to some of us: some people are born Queer or Genderqueer and Scripture even supports that idea. This is true whether your tradition supports sexual and gender identity of all expressions, or you view non-heterosexual and non-cisgender individuals as living in sin.

For those in more conservative churches, let me start with two important truths: first, God, in holy perfection, created all things and all people (Gen 1:1—2:4). Secondly, Scripture also identifies sexual practice outside of the marriage of a man and a woman to be sinful (Gen 19:1-7; Lev 17-20; Judg 19; Rom 1:18-32; and 1 Cor 6:9-20). Yet, some people are born into a body that their minds and souls do not perceive to align with as the right gender. How can the experiences of so many align with the truth of God's word?

The view of sin as distorting everything in this world to a broken image of our intended place and interactions with creation allows for space in this difficult conversation. This is not to say that people are the embodiments of sin, but that every single aspect of creation is affected by brokenness. The Wesleyan Church calls the extension of this doctrine of sin, *infirmities*—sin which affects us from birth manifesting physically, mentally, emotionally, or spiritually causing us to be vulnerable.

We can all see the way that creation has been affected by our poor care of the planet we were meant to cherish. We are also quick to recognize that some people naturally struggle with sin of one variety or another. Conservative Christians must ask the question why the line is often drawn between the accepted or expected effects of sin and the experience of an individual's sexuality/gender—especially for individuals in transition. What if this beautiful soul in front of you truly does suffer from a sense of disconnect between their intended gender and the body into which they were born?

Suicide is already far too prevalent in the Queer community. They do not need believers to further exacerbate their pain by saying that the feelings and experiences they go through are not real—or that they have chosen to endure this pain willingly. Instead of dismissing an individual's identity as attention seeking behavior as has sometimes been suggested by the church, choose to admit that sin exists in this world. Sin that could have affected a child before they were born causing their genitalia to form inconsistently with God's will.

This is not a defeatist, overly liberal attitude, but instead a gospel-minded attitude towards individuals. God does not make mistakes, but sin affects every aspect of life. Our world is broken from the image that God first intended. Why would we ever think that the humanity's first sin—which changed the role of Adam and Eve from their intended partnership to subjugation—did not affect gender and sexual identity?

I pray that if you hear nothing else in this chapter, you hear this: we cannot assume we fully understand the lives of others. Each person is affected by their unique traumas, hardships, joys, dreams, and lives within their sphere of life experience. Nothing gives us the right to erase those moments in their lives with our assumptions. In likeness to the ministry of Christ, I pray that we stop and see each person within their context *before* we try to speak to their needs.

CHAPTER 7

Things to Avoid in Ministering to Family and Friends

Identifying Community-Killers in High-Stakes Relationships

Zach did not want to reject his faith, or say that God made a mistake, but his family could not perceive any other reason for his change of identity than selfish embrace of sin. His family refused to acknowledge that he was going through big changes in his life. To them, *he* would always and forever be *she*. In their eyes, God did not make mistakes, and for Zach to go through transition was the highest insult to the creator God they all loved and served.

Their perceptions of his change led them to make harsh decisions that were unwarranted and deeply scarring to everyone involved. They used their faith as their weapon of choice. Zach now lives on the other side of the country and has no contact with his birth family *or his faith.*

How do you minister when the stakes are highest? What do you say to your sibling, friend, or child? How do you show them love and give them dignity if your perspective of faith teaches you that their choices do not align with God's will? We will talk about some practical examples of that in chapter 10, but for now, you need to stop committing these three mistakes that can kill your relationship with your loved ones.

Interventions

Common Example: Family/Friend Interventions

Why this kills community: This type of confrontation distances vulnerable individuals from a potential source of love and support, encouraging them to find support wherever they can.

Interventions have long been a practice in conservative Christian homes in which a loved one experiences a change of sexual or gender identity. This type of intervention can be described as an attempt to *set a person straight* by the family expressing their fears, disappointments, and anger to the person targeted. Interventions are often emotionally charged and result in hurts, mistrust, and shame for all involved.

When we try to discuss sexual identity with the same old "we can't allow sin in the camp" approach, we set ourselves (and our loved ones) up for failure. While a person may respond and even recognize their practices are not in line with a biblical precedent for sex, their perception will always be stained by distance. Holy division from sin in the camp does nothing but drive more people to hell.

When our focus targets the sin of the individual, we make their journey of faith all about removing what is wrong with them. It is important that we each come to realize that there are areas of our lives that do not reflect the holiness of God. Interventions and targeted approaches like this fail to offer the most important part of the gospel—the balance of truth and love of God as we offer the divine extension of grace to others.

It can be argued that interventions are performed out of love for the individual, but it is not the *intent* behind how we minister that is being called into question here. As individuals, we must be aware of how our actions will be perceived by those we are trying to help and give support. Interventions are perceived in the same way as a 12-step group or conversion therapy.

This type of response leads to our loved ones to ask themselves questions like, "*Why would my family think that I am as dangerous as an untreated alcoholic or methamphetamine addict?*" Interventions are community-killers because they create a perception that each individual must conform to our set of standards or get out.

This caution also applies to the circumstances of our families of faith. While pastors in non-affirming traditions may feel led to address what is seen as dangerous sinful practice, it can cause individuals to feel targeted if they are not in a place where they desire change in their lives. Forcing correction—which is often related to Paul's New Testament approaches to safeguarding the community from those who willfully engage in sin—can easily become an act of conversion therapy.

Rather than an intervention, allow the individual to bring their situation to you and ask for your help. It is far too dangerous to embrace corrective ministries without extreme caution and the willingness of the individual. Should that not take place, and your concerns for the greater community become critical—such as the individual wants to begin teaching or practicing things other than what your interpretation of Scripture allows—utilize the principles of Matt 18.

> If another member of the church sins against you, go and point out the fault when the two of you are alone. If the member listens to you, you have regained that one. But if you are not listened to, take one or two others along with you, so that every word may be confirmed by the evidence of two or three witnesses. If the member refuses to listen to them, tell it to the church; and if the offender refuses to listen even to the church, let such a one be to you as a Gentile and a tax collector. (Matt 18:15–17)

I strongly discourage this in cases of sexual and gender identity, but if you still feel compelled to practice exclusionary ministry, I beg you to practice it as a means of correcting all varieties of sin. Historically, the church has been apt to only utilize the actions of excommunication for the sins we deem to be more dangerous to our communities. If you speak to sexual misconduct, you must also be faithful to speak to gluttony, anger, abuse, lying, thievery, and all other destructive patterns of life.

You must also bear in mind that this principle from the Gospel of Matthew is not meant to correct new or nonbelievers in their faith journey. This is a process for like-minded believers who desire to remain in the same community with one another. Ultimately, Jesus loved the gentiles and the tax collectors and desired that they too would be welcomed into community.

As ministers, and loved ones, we must ask ourselves why we are choosing these patterns of correction. Are we trying to rush this process of hope and healing? Do we only embrace the principle of harmony encouraged in the Gospel of Matthew in situations that appear more volatile or dangerous to the community? Have we lost sight of why we are striving for restoration to one another?

We must also be mindful that there is nothing wrong with interpreting Scripture according to our unique hermeneutics—so long as we all remain faithful to orthodoxy. While some Christians read Scripture and perceive that sexual misconduct includes all Queer practice, others read Scripture and interpret it as permissive. The correction pattern of Matt 18 may simply serve as a bridge for you to realize that another church may better serve the individual to whom you are ministering.

More likely than not, the person confronted will choose the community that loves them for who they are as an individual over the community that says they are not good enough. I am not saying that conservative believers must change their interpretations of Scripture—unique hermeneutics and understandings of God's Word add to the mosaic of our faith. What is imperative is that we must all prioritize our view of the importance of each individual and give each person the dignity they deserve.

Fear and Silence

Common Example: Remaining Silent

Why this kills community: Silence creates opportunity for others to determine what we think about our neighbors—and it is not typically perceived as love.

It is easy to stay silent when you do not know what to say in a particular situation. Sometimes this practice can be a good thing, but when it comes to issues of oppression or identity, silence can be a weapon. By not speaking, we allow others to impose their impressions on us, or even speak for us. We create opportunities for violence to happen, and we create further distance between God and humanity.

Christians from more conservative perspectives stand in a difficult position theologically and relationally with those who are members of the Queer community. Conservative Christians tend to uphold the truths of Scripture in such a way that promotes cisgender heterosexual marriage as the only appropriate context for intercourse. This is held in tension with the truth that all people are welcomed in God's kingdom. Without compromising one belief or the other, is it possible to create a meaningful space for believers of all kinds? Can we create meaningful space for those who have already been ostracized by the church?

There is a hilarious photo of me as a child at a zoo on the day my grade one class met our pen pals from another school. In this photo, three girls are standing smiling together, and there I am, off to the side—scowling. At first glance, it looks like I hate these girls and want nothing to do with them. In fact, the story behind the photo is quite the opposite of how it appears.

I can clearly recall that in the moments prior to my scowling immortalization, the girls were laughing and talking, enjoying getting to know one another. I had never seen the show they were talking about and felt excluded. When it was time for the photo to be taken, no one told me that I was supposed to be included. I was feeling heartbroken and rejected. I just assumed that since the teacher called out to them to take a photo, it was only for them—after all, I was not part of their conversation anymore.

If we never extend an invitation or create space for members of the Queer community to engage with faith, how will they know that they are welcomed into our family photo as children of God? When we remain silent, it is often mistaken for agreement with those who champion condemnation. Even when we don't know what to say to our loved ones who identify outside of perceived heteronormative expectations, it is better to speak in humility and love than to remain silent.

If we allow fear to keep us silent when they need to hear our loving words most, our fear will drive our loved ones out of our homes and into hell. "For God did not give us a spirit of cowardice, but rather a spirit of power and of love and of self-discipline" (1 Tim 1:7). God is with us and will help us to see the needs of our loved ones when we are faithful in using our voice.

Fear and Anxiety

Common Example: Worst-Case Scenario Views of Sexual Identity

Why this kills community: When we allow fear to influence our perception of another's sexual identity, we can quickly link sexual identity to criminality (for example, the thought that divergent sexual identities, such as homosexuality or pansexuality, lead to pedophilia or bestiality).

There is a scene in the classic fairy tale of "Beauty and the Beast" in which Belle reveals the kind, wonderful beast to others as a means of trying to vindicate her father from suspected lunacy. All the townspeople see in the magic mirror is a monster. They cannot see the kindness or care of the beast that Belle has known. They instantly assume things about the beast and rally the town to go kill him—to save the children from the horrible danger he poses. This danger did not exist until their fear told them it did, and blinded them from anything that might tell them otherwise.

As a child raised in a conservative church denomination, I heard my share of monster stories about the Queer community. It was a belief spoken by many mouths in many places that one type of sexual divergence would certainly lead to another. The caution would be given that universally, you should be cautious of anyone who is not heterosexual. The reasoning was that if they could choose a partner outside of heteronormative standards, it was inevitable that permitting homosexuality would lead to the normalizing of bestiality or pedophilia as well.

Let's pause for a moment. This "extension of sexual depravities" teaching did not come from Scripture, but instead emerged from the sharp fears of the Cold War. This was a simple teaching that was meant to help you find out which of your neighbors were secretly communist. This type of fear boils down misinformation and transforms it into weaponry. It is a teaching that belongs in Jedi temples, not our churches.

The best way to distance yourself from this kind of fear is to get more information and ask questions. Learn the reasons why your family member or friend has come to this conclusion about their sexuality. Asking questions is a way to keep the conversation open and show your loved one that you ultimately still love them.

We must check our facts and the sources of your information on sexuality. Are these sources considered credible? Consult the Scriptures frequently and discern if there are differences in what Scripture teaches and what you have believed they said. Do the two align, or have you implied things that are not explicitly said? Our immersion in solid information and the Word of God will strengthen our ability to support our loved ones. Like a child who fears the monsters under the bed, shining a light and learning the truth can dissipate our reasons to fear.

Failure

Common Error: Openly Mourning "What Could Have Been" Long Term

Why this kills community: In repeatedly expressing your mourning, it can destabilize your relationship and cause your loved one to belief that you view them only as a disappointment.

Have you ever experienced a conversation with a person that was intensely passive-aggressive? Was that person someone that you honestly wanted to continue a relationship with? My guess is that that conversation left you feeling exhausted, beaten down, and less than excited to see them again.

Grief is natural when something expected is lost to you and is an important natural process. However, there is a type of grief that creates a failure culture that will kill community. Grieving in a passive-aggressive or self-centered manner will restrict your chances to connect with your loved ones.

If we place this conversation outside of the conversation of sexual and gender identity for a moment, the destructive nature of this grief can become clear. Imagine that your parents saw you and your spouse were struggling to conceive children for nearly a decade. What if they met that intense pain and longing with grief that sounded like this, "I thought I would be a grandmother by now," "It's not that hard to have a baby," or, "I'll be dead by the time you have children." Imagine how painful it would be to have your personal pain or struggle become all about another person's needs or desires—a grievance they renewed at every opportunity. If we look at this example and step back into the conversation of sexual and gender identity, there are some striking similarities to commonplace reactions of even the most embracing families. Those coming out as Queer in a conservative Christian home are often met by the destructive grief of their loved ones.

As I said, grief is natural, and can even be healthy to express in the conversation with your relationships with members of the Queer community. Initial or short-term grief is allowable in these situations because unlike long-term/self-centered/passive-aggressive grief, it is understandable that when life changes there is an adjustment period. When grief extends, it creates a failure culture that not only speaks of the distance created between you, but also to your failure to recognize the importance of their choices and journey through life. The extension of open grieving ultimately communicates the image of failure onto your loved one.

You cannot live in destructive grief and communicate the love of Christ. When you choose to communicate open and extended grief, your relationship becomes the source of toxic love, and pushes your loved ones away from you. You create distance by placing your own priorities and needs above theirs. When someone views you as less important—simply by the way they talk about your life—you will likely feel less of an incentive to remain in community with them.

PART THREE

Ministries That Make a Difference

CHAPTER 8

In the Image of Christ

Creating Genuine Christian Communities and Disciples

The Importance of Identity in Christ

I have been teaching on matters of sexual identity and inclusion for more than ten years. Over the years, I have often been asked one particularly telling question, "But if members of the Queer community are fully welcomed to participate in our churches, won't that limit or tarnish our gospel message?" Each time I have received this question, my response has been the same: "Who exactly are we preaching the gospel for?"

Looking at our general church practices, we must be attentive to the needs of others (regardless of what lifestyle they bring with them). Welcoming all people to participate in the faith does not inherently stain the message of hope that we offer. Does the attendance of sinners in our churches hurt the message that sinners have a place in God's kingdom through the blood of Jesus Christ?

To practice a faithful and gospel-centered ministry, inclusion must be considered as essential. This being said, many conservative pastors have expressed a sense of unease with certain aspects of inclusion because there is confusion over the possibility of inclusion being mistaken with their endorsing of lifestyles to which they do not agree. In welcoming all people, we are accomplishing our task and commission as believers. If the gospel was not meant to be offered to all people, Peter never would have experienced his rooftop vision in Acts 10:9–22.

Cornelius was praying as a "God-fearing man" (Acts 10:22) which in the eyes of the Jewish Sanhedrin was barely better than being a godless pagan. When Cornelius found God during honest prayer and searching, Peter's willingness to embrace him and his family was the game changer. Cornelius *begged* to hear the truth of the gospel. It was in this explanation of his hope that Peter proclaims, "I now realize how true it is that God does not show favoritism but accepts men from every nation who fear him and do what is right" (Acts 10:34–35).

We must recognize our role in offering grace. Peter had his vision and immediately went to Cornelius' home and invited them to share in the hope of God. Based on what we understand of common Roman religious/ceremonial practices, Cornelius was not living according to Jewish standards or doing everything right. He did what he knew was right, and God interceded to help Cornelius and his family with the rest.

Why are we more likely to act like the Jewish Sanhedrin than the early church? God gave Israel ten primary commandments to uphold and follow. Ultimately, the Jewish community upheld more than six hundred laws as a means of prohibiting even the remote possibility of breaking the Ten Commandments. The desire for obedience was genuine, but living under the fear of breaking these laws did nothing to keep them from deviating from God's will.

In the New Testament, Jesus challenged the idea of Sabbath laws as held by the community and ultimately questioned whether these laws were truly God's. Christ encouraged all followers to love God in a liberated way, a way that included even the Samaritans. This is the difference of the New Testament and the Old

Testament—encouragement to practice healthy inclusive faith over unhealthy prohibition-based faith.

When we approach Scripture with transformation and encouragement in mind, we foster the growth of healthy individuals and infuse them with the love of Christ. As a superior alternative to focusing on preventing or removing sin, focusing on a positive and transformative aspect of their identity creates a natural means of inclusion. Offering inclusion to Cornelius—a pagan—transformed the lives and hearts of his whole family forever.

This process is so inclusive because it fosters intimacy and dispels isolation within the community. When every person is encouraged to find their identity in Christ, the things which can naturally divide our communities—race, politics, sex—no longer have the right to take the center stage of our attention (Gal 3:28). Christ alone holds the center of our hearts and unites us where the isolation of focusing on sin removal drives us apart.

Ministries and Practices That Reinforce Identity: Discipleship as Mentoring

Common Opportunity: Intentional Discipleship Groups/Mentoring

Why it builds community: When individuals participate in life groups/identity-forming groups, it establishes a sense of communal identity rather than alienating them by focusing on prohibitions.

While discipleship groups or spiritual mentoring groups will often address personal growth issues, they should not become overly focused on any particular aspect of an individual's life. When discipleship becomes overly specific in group settings, it can hinder other major areas of needed spiritual growth. This approach would be like a trauma surgeon fixing a broken leg when there a tear in a major artery.

If you are approaching this from a more conservative background, you may be thinking, *"But isn't sexual and gender identity a major issue that should be addressed?"* It is not our place to decide what issue is the most important for a person to tackle first when growing in holiness. The Holy Spirit will lead and guide believers in their pursuit of growth—personal beliefs (even those rooted in your understanding of Scripture) cannot be allowed to supersede God's perfect work and timing.

Identity is not an issue that divides a person into another category of need for personal discipleship. In other words, you do not need to have a Queer background to shepherd a Queer Christian. The sexual and gender expressions of the discipleship group members are not determining factors for the process of becoming more like Christ.

This is not to say that these things are completely irrelevant to the partnerships that we form in our small group settings. Mentors and leaders must be aware of the needs of each disciple in their groups and strive to build an understanding of the soil in which their faith is growing. Knowing where each of our identities currently rest allows us to have better insights into how we can help growth and be aware of what challenges we may face as we walk together.

Being raised in a farming community, I learned that if you know what kind of soil you have, it helps you better care for the plants you are trying to grow. You can determine what fertilizers to use, how much water to give, and even how to build up the soil around your plants. Our faith journeys must also be carefully fertilized, watered, and built up. Knowing that Queer Christians have a unique soil (as we each do), we as leadership must learn about the general needs of the Queer community. Here are a few simple ways we can better equip ourselves to serve the members of our community:

1. **Be willing to learn about the unique cultural experiences of each individual.** What language defines their understandings of life, love, and happiness? Does Queer culture use common language differently than you do? Are there terms used in Queer culture that are unfamiliar to you? What are the basic tenets of Queer culture that align with the gospel? Which ones differ? You may be surprised where Queer culture and Scripture intersect and unite.

2. **Be understanding that the Holy Spirit will be the one to reveal areas of growth to them.** To those of more conservative positions on the matter, be prepared for the possibility that sexual or gender identity may not be something that God brings to their attention. Are you willing to work with them in their pursuit of holiness as they listen to the Holy Spirit's prompting? A good section of Scripture to keep in mind to help us engage in this kind of humility as leaders is Matt 7:3–5. When we allow the Holy Spirit to lead us and our siblings in the faith, we can truly seek holiness together.

The good news is that you probably already have a ministry in your church that is built—or ready—to take on this role. Unlike the targeted ministries which we addressed in chapter 5, this mentoring or use of small groups would be non-specific to the Queer community. Instead, participation would focus on a shared interest in personal growth to help establish a healthy new pattern of life that centers on Christ. The life groups/Bible studies most churches already have can be an excellent place in which we can create a safe space for people to find their identity in Christ.

Identifying Inconsistent Theologies and Establishing Consistent Theologies and Practices

Even if we do have these types of ministries in place, there must be intentional shifts in our thinking and practices in order to fully create an inclusive community. To truly focus on building a healthy identity in Christ, we must identify our inconsistencies and create consistent healthy practices. Developing a well-formed, well-rounded teaching pattern establishes a communal identity in a much healthier manner than providing the list of prohibitions.

Many churches and families have taken an absentee approach to creating and utilizing catechisms. The strength of intentional teachings on faith lies in their ability to identify areas in which our practice does not align with our beliefs. New and young believers will learn what we genuinely believe by how we practice our faith—words are just words if we do not practice them. What scriptural and cultural practices are we passing on? Are we proud of the legacy that we are creating? If the community that we are creating does not reflect the love of Christ and encourage believers to grow, then we are fostering faith within an inconsistent theology.

It is hard to identify where these inconsistencies lie if we are not actively engaging our faith in a set pattern of teaching. To develop a catechism can be a large undertaking, but doing so creates patterns and rhythms of growth in our faith communities and lives. Determine what core values, faith principles, and beliefs matter most so that you can ensure that discipleship is balanced. As a means of offering help so that you can instill a firm foundation of faith, here are two guiding principles to consider.

Do you encourage positive change and growth, while being drawn to and relying on negative Scriptures, teachings, and theologies?

Many churches are great at talking about their commitment to the teaching and practice of holiness and hope, but what Scriptures do we tend to turn to when expressing our beliefs? While all Scripture is God-breathed and useful (2 Tim 3:16–17), we must acknowledge that not every Scripture is suited to teach every lesson equally.

If we teach a practice or belief by only utilizing negative examples from Scriptures, it can lead to fears and anxieties over committing wrongdoings—rather than encouraging health and holiness. Think of the doctor's visits in which you receive lists and lists of things which you can no longer enjoy. Do you feel encouraged to practice healthy living? If you do, what is motivating your journey to health—hope or fear of a worsening diagnosis?

When we compare the Ten Commandments in Exodus 20:1–17, there is a very different feel than what we read in Matthew 22:36–40. Both of these Scriptures communicate the important practices of loving God and others, but they do so from very distinct perspectives. One speaks from the lens of restrictions, and the other communicates from a lens of love and hope.

If we only teach Exodus 20:1–17 without a context of love, our theology becomes inconsistent. A consistent way to teach these sorts of negative Scriptures would be to share them in light of the hope of Christ. When we move from a negative perspective into a perspective of hope, we can use Scriptures of all sorts to imbue hope and develop strong foundations for healthy disciples.

Do you communicate that the gospel is for all people, but use exclusionary language?

Generally, there are three questions by which we can begin to reveal a problem if it exists within our community.

1. What do our life groups/small groups focus on?
2. What do we preach about?
3. Is our church happy?

Think about the last year in your community. How many groups have focused on practical living guides from a negative perspective? How many times has your sermon point been rebuking a negative behavior or practice? Does your congregation genuinely seem to love one another, or do you tend to see socially appropriate smiles? If you only ever offer teaching on how to avoid the pitfalls of sin, but never encourage right living, it will show.

Preaching holiness is not limited to avoiding sin. In fact, how you preach can remain mostly the same—just change the tone in which you develop your points. As we have talked about, the Ten Commandments all use negative language, but when Christ summarizes them into the Greatest Commandments, positive language is used extensively. Negative phrases discourage unity in the body of believers, and it discourages individuals from finding their identity in Christ. It is easier to develop an identity like Christ when you focus on the good things that create that identity instead of all the sins that prevent it.

The use of negative language also disconnects us from the message of Christ as the hope of the world. Imagine if you showed up at work and your boss is praising the team for their excellent work in going beyond the month's sales quota. What if in the same breath he then chastised the team about all the other sales that *could* have been made?

That is the kind of tension that often exists in our churches without us noticing. We talk about the hope of Jesus' birth at Christmas, but by Easter, many churches are focusing only on how our evil ways nailed him to the cross. These things are both true, but they appear inconsistent to the hope of Christ. How we present the gospel matters as much as what we believe about salvation.

Within your community, embrace language and practices that welcome all people to the table. Is it out of the question to say the word *partner* instead of spouse/wife/husband when talking about marriage? Without changing your definition of biblical marriage, you can use language that embraces every variety of couple that attends.

A few years ago, Nix shared with me that they chose to stop going to their church because there was never anything there for them. None of the messages that had been shared or small groups offered them anything that *they* could use. The problem was not that God's truth was not shared in a specific way, but rather that God's truth had been so specialized for the rest of community that it alienated their own needs as an individual. When we share God's word with a focus on building identity in such a way that is attainable to all, we enable real transformation in our community.

CHAPTER 9

Creating a Culture of Intimacy

The Importance of Normalizing Celibacy

About ten years ago, Jonas expressed in passing that he no longer felt he could attend his church and was seeking another to be his home. Out of pastoral habit, I asked if he had a particular reason for his choice to leave the community he had been established in for many years. His response was that every adult ministry he tried to connect with left him feeling like he was only half of a person—even the ministry geared toward men had a focus on being a husband.

His experience with these ministries left as much of a hole as it helped to fill. He certainly felt the love of God and grew in his faith, but he began to experience a deep sense of pain over a failed marriage. Ultimately, his disconnect was so great that he felt it was important to find a community which offered something to singles other than a single-and-ready-to-mingle ministry.

Experiences like this are repeated in many churches—we try to offer ministries that foster healthy families, but we fail to offer anything to those who do not have a *traditional* family. Whether single parent, divorced, unmarried, cohabitating/common-law, Genderqueer, or Queer person, the pressure of the church to fit within a certain mold line can create undue stress. So how can we minister to a full assortment of families?

It is our responsibility to create space for all of God's children to experience transformative and hope-filled love. Scripture reinforces the importance of not placing stumbling blocks in front of the youngest in the faith, and preventing them from experiencing the hope of the gospel in their lives. When our faith and practices centralize on marriage or engendered experiences, we run an enormous risk of placing millstones that become tombstones.

The Importance of Normalizing Celibacy

Even within the Wesleyan Church, a church which has been founded on egalitarian beliefs, there exists a tension surrounding marriage and singleness. Many communities seem to venerate marriage above singleness—and singles are often met with questions regarding their hopes for marriage and dating life. We may preach that we believe all people are created equal, but we sometimes act as though couples are better at fulfilling the mission of God.

Perhaps this unconsciously stems from our teachings on the creation of humanity? Has it accidentally become our viewpoint that offering celibacy ministries denies the creation mandate (Gen 1:26–28)? As we offer ministries to our churches, we must consider the interpretation of what it meant to "be fruitful and multiply" (Gen 1:28). When we promote the view that celibacy is inadequate in our communities, are we forgetting the meaning of "the Creation Mandate . . . in light of the person of Jesus Christ—his birth, life, death, resurrection, and coming return?"[1] Perhaps to view the text of Gen 1:26–28 as a *biological* creation mandate is far too narrow a view—considering that Christ as a single, celibate human fulfilled this very mandate in how he cared for God's kingdom.

Celibacy should be a staple teaching and practice in our communities of faith—as it reminds us that our incompleteness is not fulfilled in the joining of a second incomplete partner. Soul mates are not a biblical idea, and we must stop acting as if marriage fixes

1. Hitchcock, *Significance of Singleness*, 40.

the sinful nature of an individual. When we establish this teaching as a normative practice in our churches, it can ease the transition of those who are not heterosexual, gender binary, or in committed relationships into our communities.

This practice can help individuals experience invitation regardless of our perspectives on matters of identity. This transition is eased by creating space for individuals to flourish as individuals without the added pressure of finding their other half. Our attempts to enable healthy families should never come at the cost of someone else's invitation and approach to faith.

Creating an Invitational Culture by Normalizing Celibacy

The main tool we can use in our attempt to creature a culture that welcomes the practice of celibacy is the normalization of our language towards marriage and the family. Paul was incredibly effective at creating this balance in his New Testament writings. For all that we see of his writings in the book of Ephesians to familial households (Eph 5:21—6:9), we also see his encouragements to singletons to remain celibate and pursue a life of liberty to serve the gospel (1 Cor 7:32–34).

We must create space in our congregations for people to approach the throne of God without hindrance. I cannot overstate the depth of importance of our inclusion of celibacy language and practices in our communities for the reception and retention of Queer converts—especially for churches that hold more conservative beliefs.

When we decentralize our use of matrimonial language, the conversation can move away from sexual obstacles to participation in faith and onto the importance of forming an identity in Christ. When we remove the expectations of marriage as the endgame, all believers are welcomed to the throne of God. As Christians, we become empowered to minister to those who do not fit within biblical paradigms of relationships.

While we should continue to give encouragement and spiritual guidance to those in relationships, we must be careful not to be overly specific in our language to general audiences. When we uphold the importance of holy life in marriage, we must also promote the potential for joy and holy life in celibacy. Ultimately, we must be attentive to the needs and identities of all believers.

Our goal should be to create an intimate culture in our community that invites all people to pursue God. In becoming vulnerable in how we extend our invitation to others, a culture of intimacy will naturally take root. Spiritual intimacy and vulnerability will empower others to engage with the Holy Spirit and one another more deeply.

Jonas shared his difficult search for community with his former pastoral team, but found no resolution in any of the offered groups or ministries of his longtime church. If there had simply been space for him as a single person to worship God—without the expectation of eventually becoming a spouse—he would have stayed at his church. He now attends a church that supports him in his contentment of a single, celibate lifestyle.

Jonas was a heterosexual man who simply did not have a wife. Imagine how much harder it would have been for him to find space in that community if he had been a gay or transgendered man who also felt the pressure of not meeting implied heteronormative standards? Would he have even sought out another church family? Normalizing celibacy in our churches can create intimacy and help believers develop a firm foundation in Christ.

Ministries and Practices That Reinforce Intimacy

Recognizing that there is an importance to creating a culture that embraces celibacy, we must consider the practical methods we can choose to embody our desire to create intimacy for all believers. We can build a community of intimacy most effectively by empowering our small groups to focus on the transformation of the individual within their current context.

Common Opportunity #1: Activity-Based Small Groups/Gatherings

Why it builds community: Common activities depressurize situational anxieties associated with small group settings.

When smalls groups focus on a shared activity or hobby, they introduce conversation naturally. This kind of contextual teaching establishes lasting patterns of change, as the words of Christ are set in the context in which the person already lives. By pulling the focus onto a hobby instead of onto a theme of study or the gender of participants, it creates a safe space for new believers to enter the community, and become intimate with Christ and other believers.

The goal in this kind of ministry is to establish deeply connected disciples who have the support they need to face the personal struggles that come from the natural journey of becoming more Christlike. Teaching and deeper discipleship are not excluded in this model but will take on different forms than they have previously. By taking time to consider the needs of others, you simply create space for others to enjoy life as celibate individuals.

Consider what types of retreats, gatherings, and special events your church offers. Do you offer masculine activities that women would also be welcomed to attend—or feminine activities that men would be welcomed to enjoy? This practice not only creates a healthier view of binary genders, but also removes the pressure of conforming from nonbinary and non-hetero believers and seekers.

For individuals wanting to create space for the celibacy practices of others, ask yourself these questions:

1. When you plan activities with others, are they centered on couples or gendered activities?
2. Are your first concerns for the dating lives or family-planning of your friends? Or do you focus on their interests and activities in life?

Common Opportunity #2: Sensitivity Training

Why it builds community: When you train your leaders to use sensitive language, you invite participation from all people.

Do we consider the needs of single parents? How about the needs of Queer families? Be sure to be inclusive in your familial and partnership language—and recognize the fact that not all congregants are living in a two-hetero-cis-parents situation. We must begin dialogue with others so that we as hetero-normative cisgender families can understand and support the needs of those who are not. For some individuals and communities, this may mean moving away from some of your traditional resources or practices in ministry.

Go to the bibliography of this book and pick a few of the books to read that are written from Queer perspectives. These books will highlight the needs of the Queer community and identify needs the church can easily fill. If you are from a non-affirming (or conservative) faith tradition, this will be especially important. Listening to the needs of others can often help you engage individuals whose personal identities and cultures differ widely from your own.

Another important step in this process is to connect with local Pride groups and simply ask the question: "*What are your needs?*" Stepping out like this may feel uncomfortable, but we were not called to be comfortable. Jesus often met physical needs before addressing spiritual considerations. When we recognize needs, we are better equipped to support our greater community with the hope and love of Jesus Christ.

CHAPTER 10

The Importance of the Individual

Making Space for What Matters Most

O Lord, you have searched me and known me. You know when I sit down and when I rise up; you discern my thoughts from far away. You search out my path and my lying down, and are acquainted with all my ways. Even before a word is on my tongue, O Lord, you know it completely. You hem me in, behind and before, and lay your hand upon me. . . . For it was you who formed my inward parts; you knit me together in my mother's womb. I praise you, for I am fearfully and wonderfully made. Wonderful are your works; that I know very well. My frame was not hidden from you, when I was being made in secret, intricately woven in the depths of the earth. Your eyes beheld my unformed substance. In your book were written all the days that were formed for me, when none of them as yet existed.

—Ps 139:1–5, 13–16

A common thread in each of the stories that I have felt impelled to share in this book has been that Queer/celibate congregants did not feel as though they had value within the eyes of the church. In their interviews, many expressed that they would hear phrases about loving the sinner, but not the sin, or other trite phrases that only served to emphasis what divided them from the community. It seemed to these diverse North American individuals as though the church could never just leave the dialogue at: *Jesus loves you.* There was always something added to the love of Christ that cheapened their experience of faith.

Why is it that we are so afraid to embrace God's children as they are? Is it fear of the steeply dysfunctional North American view of individualism? Let's talk about that fear for a moment. In placing importance on the individual's journey towards Christ, we are not giving in to a postmodern or "me-first" culture. Rather, we are deeply instilling the presence of Christ in their lives.

If the journey of the individual was not an important aspect of our faith, we would not have Scriptures such as Ps 139 which describe the enormous value of each person in God's eyes. If the church does not allow for the individual to flourish, we run the risk of losing our identities completely. The church must be the place in which we set the tone for how we *showcase* the individual.

Recognizing and Valuing the Journey of Each Person towards Christ

In our lives, we each face the journey of learning who we are as individuals. This is an essential part of our growth in relationship with God and with one another. We learn about ourselves, so that we can learn about the presence of God in our lives. This process is a staple experience for every person as they discern not only their individuality, but their sexual and gender identities.

Our choices in language and decor can communicate our positions loudly. When we use language such as the colloquial phrase "love the sinner, hate the sin," we risk communicating that the *basis* of a person's identity is not good enough. When we label our facilities with binary bathrooms, we communicate *only* binary genders are welcome. When families and friends refuse to identify their loved one by their preferred pronouns or respond with disbelief, we remind our loved one that they are not the same—they do not meet our expectations.

Those who do not identify as cisgender, binary, and/or heterosexual often experience this additional stress when navigating the unfamiliar. Being "consistently called into question can lead to isolation, but it can also lead to startling connections with people who do *not* call you into question."[1] People notice when the pressure to make public identity choices is removed, and they often feel more comfortable returning to these spaces. Wouldn't it be incredible if we as Christians offered those startling connections that could offer hope and love?

Ministries and Practices That Reinforce the Individual

If our faith is founded on the hope of transformation for each individual, why would we ever act as though the experience of each and every person was not essential? A person is made of many parts, and when we ignore sexual and gender identity, we lose sight of the individuals to whom we are called to minister.

Common Opportunity #1: Embrace the Testimonies of Every Individual

Why it builds community: When there is diversity in the voices that are speaking about their journeys with God, more individuals feel welcomed to join that process.

We must understand that "the individual's profound value to the Creator and Savior is a biblical notion."[2] While we have not always correctly situated the importance of the individual in the community of believers, we must strive to listen to the stories and

1. Airton, *Gender: Your Guide*, 41.

2. Harper and Metzger, *Exploring Ecclesiology*, 40.

experiences of all people. Testimonies serve to bring balance to the tension of upholding the personal and communal needs.

Do we create the space necessary for individuals in our communities to hold up the stories of their lives and say God has brought me this far? If space is not adequately given to each person to encounter God *as they are,* they will never have the chance to learn *who they could be.*

Hearing and sharing experiences of faith can also serve to link our community together in ways that we could not begin to anticipate. It has been reported that many transgender women and infertile women (or who have suffered pregnancy loss) find similarities in their experiences of womanhood due to the cultural expectations of maternity.[3] When we place value on the individual, we can see similar bridges built through our process of learning to care for each other as individuals.

Common Opportunity #2: Encourage Growth in Christ

Why it builds community: When we place an emphasis on the spiritual disciplines and growth, it decentralizes our focus on sins/differences and centralizes our pursuit of holiness.

By placing emphasis on spiritual growth there is naturally attention given to the growth of the individual. In maintaining the uniqueness of the person, disciples can be more firmly rooted in both their communal and person identity. Encourage individuals and your small groups to engage with books like Richard Foster's *Celebration of Discipline,* Jarod Osborne's *Jaded Faith,* or Howard and William D. Hendricks' *Living By the Book.* When people are equipped for personal spiritual growth, their faith becomes prioritized in and molded to their lives.

---

3. Airton, *Gender: Your Guide,* 38–42.

Common Opportunity #3: Celebrate Uniqueness through the Language You Use

Why it builds community: Much like a testimony, hearing unique language reminds us of the diverse kingdom of God to which we belong.

I was raised on the flannel graphs of an early 1990s Wesleyan Church. I remember very clearly that when it came time to talk about the stories of Jesus and the disciples, all twelve of the disciples were one chunk of flannel. One piece of flannel was supposed to represent twelve different people who came from vastly different backgrounds.

Nothing about this presentation celebrated the diversity of *who* God called to be disciples—it was just twelve white guys in dresses stuck together on one piece of flannel. Thankfully, the language of my Sunday school teachers taught me about how diverse the disciples were. Peter had a strong set of opinions paired with a bad temper. Judas struggled with greed in a time of poverty. Matthew had been a turncoat tax collector. They were *individuals* who made the incredible mosaic of God's children. By focusing on that which makes us special, unique, and different, we teach that the mosaic presentation of our communities of faith matters.

When we create space in our language for each individual to feel at home, we become a source of liberation and transformation in our community. The whitewashing/hetero-normalizing faith that swept North American culture in the early and mid-1900s does not make the gospel accessible to all people. How do you preach to partners/spouses? Does your call to worship use gender binary language? Do you limit the opportunity for engagement simply by opening your mouth? We must strongly consider what kind of language we are willing to use in our communities to create that invitation to faith and celebrate our diversity as individuals.

Common Opportunity #4: Keep Social Media Connections Alive

Why this builds community: Analogue friendships are seen as the ones who you are ashamed of or to which you are not totally committed.

Consider what your social media is communicating to others. No one is forcing you to share or repost the things that others put on their social media accounts. What might seem humorous to you may grieve others. The choice to engage in groups with inflammatory messages can prevent people from hearing you share the gospel.

Likewise, the choice of some Christians to completely disconnect on socials from their Queer friends/family can communicate the same things. There is no shame in being friends with those who identify as Queer. Shame exists in the moments we choose to act in ways that isolate others from the love of Jesus Christ. Once these lines of communication are broken, there will be no way to fully repair the damage that has been done.

Conclusion

How we minister matters. As we consider ministry and theological standpoints, we must focus less on exclusion, and instead ignite the hope of inclusion. Biblical community is not founded on fear, but on inclusion through the unity of truth and love. Our approach to the Scriptures must reflect these important desires for inclusion.

Our history of ministry has not been faultless. Before ministering to the Queer community, we must accept the fault of the church in this, and our need for humility, as we (and our forebearers) have tarnished the image of Christ. We have participated in cruelty by direct actions, indirect choices, and most egregiously, by our silence.

Our churches, ministers, and families have each been found guilty of killing the very sense of community we desire to create and offer. While our intentions have been good, we are at fault for creating painful situations. It is our responsibility to recognize and be willing to correct these errors in our ministry/relational practices.

In placing value on the individual within our cultures of intimacy and identity, we show a small glimpse of the kind of community within which we have been called to create and participate. Ultimately the goal is to create a God-honoring community that is driven by the desire to become more like Christ without sanitizing the cultures and lifestyles that our congregants are being transformed within and are actively transforming.

I have hope that we, as ministers and individuals, can see all of God's children find welcome and embrace within our churches. I have hope that the stories I have shared in this book—steeped in pain and exclusion—would not be repeated in the lives of our children and loved ones. I have hope that we can do better.

I have hope for the family who, in the fall of 2008, were forced to move out of the area by their relentless acts of violence and hatred committed by the local Christian community towards their *teenage* daughter who identified as lesbian.

I have hope for the child who, in 2009, was told by their Christian mother that they were no longer welcomed in their home because they decided to embrace a gender identity that did not match their birth sex.

I have hope for the young woman who, on Christmas Eve 2011, was outed by her mentor and pastor—for the sake of protecting others from her queerness, and her ongoing struggles with depression.

I have hope for the parent who worried that their child would face hate because they were struggling to understand their identity within a binary system of gender.

I have hope for the one who moved thousands of miles away from their Christian family that had more interest in *deadnaming* them than showing them the love of the God they loved.

I have hope for the ones who cried in my arms after I gave seminars on the topic of sexual and gender identity, and expressed the fear they had over trying to walk through their identity with their Church family and pastors.

I have hope for the child who lived as a closet gay, instead of finding the support he needed within his church and family.

I have hope for the one who confessed to me that he had to hide his testimony of coming to know Christ as it involved coming out about his transition because his church told him if he shared about his journey he could no longer serve or attend.

I have hope for the ones who have felt a pang of fear when I shared my profession as a pastor because of past hurts in their lives.

I have hope for the Gay Village in British Colombia, Canada that suffered yet another hurt on August 24th, 2020, when a pastor chose to defend the gospel from sinners by breaking the leg of a prominent sportscaster who challenged his perception of God's love.

I have hope for every individual who felt *less than*, because we—*like slavers*—have used the gospel to justify our actions.

I have hope.

Questions for Personal Reflection

Part 1: Setting the Stage for Informed Ministries

Chapter 1: Sexual Identity and the Church

1. Am I aware of the history that exists within my context between the church and Queer culture?
2. We can often interpret current relations as a reflection of historical interactions. Is my understanding of history based on assumption or genuine information?
3. How do I perceive inclusion? What does that look like? Is the term unsettling?
4. Does inclusion water down the gospel, or present it more clearly?

Chapter 2: Transforming Our Vision of Responsibility

1. The Wesleyan Church, as a denomination, stands on a foundation of their commitment to social justice. Does a commitment such as this make a Christian culpable to care for *all* of God's children?
2. What does my church look like today? Are Queer Christians represented and welcomed as beloved children of God? If there are no Queer Christians in my church, do I think they

would be welcomed if they did begin to attend? How would my church family respond?

3. Consider the language of your worship and your community. Does any language or teaching exist in my church that may prevent others from receiving the Gospel message due to abrasive presentation?

4. Have I ever considered the needs that exist in Queer communities? Does my church try to meet these needs in any way? If so, what practices and language are used? What are some ways to engage the Queer community and their unique needs?

5. Was I surprised by anything as I read through the table of Queer/Genderqueer terminology? List a few terms that I would like to learn more about.

Chapter 3: Approaching the Scriptures in Humility

1. How do I approach Scripture? Have I ever considered the ways in which others may look at God's word?

2. Sometimes, our methods of using Scripture can fluctuate as we discern God's will in various areas. Does my hermeneutic— or method of interpretation—change as I consider different topics? How do I approach subjects of divorce, the sabbath, spiritual gifts, and sexual/gender identity?

3. If I believe that Scripture labels binary gender non-conformity, and hetero-normative non-conformity as sinful practices, am I willing to minister to and with those who believe otherwise? If I am a believer that views gender and sexual expressions as a part of creation's mosaic, how can I foster unity between the Queer community and the church?

Chapter 4: Building a Biblical Community

1. Does my church community align with the view of community in the Gospel of John?

2. If "love is a question of how one deliberately walks" as Bruce Schuchard shares, then what does my daily life communicate to others?

3. Was there a passage of Scripture that challenged me as I read this chapter?

4. Exclusion is both reserved for those, and an act of bringing willful destruction into our communities. As I pursue holiness in my community, am I aware of those around me and their needs? Is my pursuit destructive to others around me?

Part 2: Avoiding Ministries That Kill Community

Chapter 5: Things to Avoid in Practical Church Ministry

1. When I see a need within my communities, do I rush to create solutions, instead of listening to those I seek to help?

2. Have I ever experienced a ministry that did more harm than good?

3. Do any of the ministries within my church focus more on removing sins, than on spiritual growth? Did these ministries begin this way, or have they shifted from their original intent?

4. Do I allow myself to become connected with those who do not align with my beliefs? Does my connection to these groups prevent others from hearing the gospel?

Chapter 6: Things to Avoid as Individuals Ministering in Our Communities

1. Have I ever witnessed public forums being used for condemnation? Am I guilty of publicly shaming others as a means of touting or displaying my own holiness?

2. Not all methods are suited well for modern culture. Are the methods of ministry I rely on antiquated forms of outreach?

Or do I strive to make the gospel accessible through means that make sense to individuals in my culture and context?

3. Do I assume to know things about individuals without considering their individual needs and situations?

Chapter 7: Things to Avoid in Ministering to Family and Friends

1. What is the reasoning behind using an intervention? Does the method serve those confronted or those performing the intervention?
2. Does fear cause me to remain silent? Have I ever held your tongue when I needed to speak? What happened as a result of my silence?
3. Fear can also lead to a deep sense of anxiety. Have I ever allowed my sense of fear and anxiety to prevent me from showing God's love to others?
4. Have I ever allowed my personal expectations to override my desire to serve and care for others?

Part 3: Ministries That Have the Potential to Make a Difference

Chapter 8: In the Image of Christ

1. Do I seek to foster a deep sense of importance for new believers to identify with Christ?
2. Do I hesitate to engage Queer Christians in our small groups and mentoring partnerships? If so, what fears/concerns/etc. are keeping me from doing so?
3. Does my church offer Christian formation classes or teachings that can help believers in growth and development? Is this available to all who attend, or only as a part of membership classes?

Chapter 9: Creating a Culture of Intimacy

1. Do I patronize the idea of celibacy, or do I engage single believers in discussion that it is a distinct and healthy possibility
   for their lives?
2. What things can I identify in my congregations and relationships that create obstacles for others to explore celibacy? Do
   I place unnecessary expectations on their lives to find a partner—regardless of gender or sexual identity? If I cannot identify obstacles, what supports am I offering to others as they
   explore their identity and possibly consider celibacy?
3. In what ways can I be more sensitive to the needs of others?
   Look through the Reference and Bibliographies to consider
   which texts may offer more training in these areas.

Chapter 10: The Importance of the Individual

1. How do I communicate that I value others? Do people know I
   am a Christ follower by how I love them?
2. Each person is on a journey of faith and has a story to share
   about their engagements in faith. Am I willing to listen and
   embrace the testimony of each individual—even when there
   may be moments that cause discomfort?
3. How can I encourage others to grow in their relationship with
   Christ and empower them to use their individual talents and
   skills?
4. The church has an incredible mosaic of believers from different cultures, backgrounds, and journeys. Am I considerate of
   the experiences of others, or do I limit my perception of a person's faith journey to what is normative in my own journey?
5. Social media can be a strange world to navigate, but it is an
   important tool as we show others that we hold them in high
   value. Do my social media accounts reflect my desire to love
   all people as precious individuals in God's sight? If not, what
   do these accounts communicate?

Bibliography

This bibliography includes many voices and many perspectives on life, faith, and morality. While not all of these voices speak from a Christian perspective, they each lend an important contribution to the conversation of how we can support one another as individuals. For Christians looking to read more about sexual and gender identity, I would encourage you to stay rooted in the discussion of identity in Scripture as you dive into this difficult discussion. May Christ lead and guide you on your journey of learning and growth.

Airton, Lee. *Gender: Your Guide*. Avon, MA: Adams Media, 2019.

Benner, David G. *Surrender to Love: Discovering the Heart of Christian Spirituality*. Downers Grove: InterVarsity, 2003.

Black, Robert, and Keith Drury. *The Story of the Wesleyan Church*. Indianapolis: Wesleyan, 2018. Kindle.

Blosnich, John R. et al. "Sexual Orientation Change Efforts, Adverse Childhood Experiences, and Suicide Ideation and Attempt Among Sexual Minority Adults, United States, 2016–2018." *American Journal of Public Health* 110 (2020) 1024–30.

Bonhoeffer, Dietrich. *Life Together: The Classic Exploration of Christian Community*. Translated by John W. Doberstein. New York: Harper One, 1954.

Burridge, Richard A. "Being Biblical? Slavery, Sexuality and the Inclusive Community." *Theology* 111 (2008) 22–31.

Cannon, Andy. *Loving the Broken: Follow God's Heart into Compassionate Living*. Indianapolis: Wesleyan, 2013.

Cusick, Jason. *Love3: Three Essentials for Making Love Last.* Indianapolis: Wesleyan, 2011.

Dadisman, MaryAnn. "Roots of Hate: Homophobia at Its Source." *Human Rights* 18 (1991): 24–25.

Deyoung, Kevin. *What Does the Bible Really Teach about Homosexuality?* Wheaton, IL: Crossway, 2015.

Dobson, James. *Marriage Under Fire: Why We Must Win This Battle.* Sisters, OR: Multnomah, 2004.

Egale Human Rights Trust. "Glossary of Terms." https://egale.ca/wpcontent/uploads/2017/03/Egales-Glossary-of-Terms.pdf Last modified March 3, 2019.

Erickson-Scroth, Laura, ed. *Trans Bodies, Trans Selves: A Resource for the Transgender Community.* New York: Oxford University Press, 2014.

Farrow, Douglas, ed. "Thirteen Theses on Marriage: Nine Scholars and Writers Respond to Pointed Propositions about Sex, Gender, and Marriage." *First Things* 226 (2012): 23–31.

"Feminist." In *The Oxford Dictionary of the Christian Church. 3rd edition*, edited by Cross, F. L. and E. A. Livingstone, 607–8. New York: Oxford University Press, 2005.

Fejes, Fred. "Murder, Perversion, and Moral Panic: The 1954 Media Campaign Against Miami's Homosexuals and the Discourse of Civic Betterment." *Journal of the History of Sexuality* 9 (2000): 305–347.

Frisby, Wendy, and Pamela Ponic. "Sport & Social Inclusion." In *Sport Policy in Canada*, edited by Lucie Thibault and Jean Harvey, 381–403. Ottawa: University of Ottawa Press, 2013.

Gagnon, Robert A. J. *The Bible and Homosexual Practice: Texts and Hermeneutics.* Nashville: Abingdon, 2001.

Gushee, David P., Brian M. McLaren, Phyllis Tickle, and Matthew Vines. *Changing Our Mind.* 2nd ed. Canton, MI: Read the Spirit, 2015.

Haines, Lee, M. and Paul Williams Thomas. *An Outline History of the Wesleyan Church.* 6th ed. Indianapolis: Wesleyan, 2005.

Harper, Brad, and Paul Louis Metzger. *Exploring Ecclesiology: An Evangelical and Ecumenical Introduction.* Grand Rapids: Brazos, 2009.

Hartke, Austin. *Transforming: The Bible and the Lives of Transgender Christians.* Louisville: Westminster John Knox, 2018.

Hawkin, David. *The Johannine World: Reflections on the Theology of the Fourth Gospel and Contemporary Society.* Albany, NY: State University of New York Press, 1996.

Hill, Wesley. *Washed and Waiting: Reflections on Christian Faithfulness and Homosexuality.* Grand Rapids: Zondervan, 2010.

Hitchcock, Christina S. *The Significance of Singleness: A Theological Vision for the Future of the Church.* Grand Rapids: Baker Academic, 2018.

Ingram, Chip. *Culture Shock: A Biblical Response to Today's Most Divisive Issues.* Grand Rapids: Baker, 2014.

Isom, Mo. *Sex, Jesus, and the Conversations the Church Forgot.* Grand Rapids: Baker, 2018.

Kelly, Benji. *Wrecked and Redeemed: Finding Hope, Freedom, and Acceptance in Christ.* Indianapolis: Wesleyan, 2018.

Kelsey, Morton T. "The Church and the Homosexual." *Journal of Religion and Health* 7 (1968): 61–78.

King, Martin Luther, Jr. *Strength to Love. 3rd edition.* Minneapolis: Fortress, 2010.

Kinsman, Gary. "'Character Weaknesses' and 'Fruit Machines': Towards an Analysis of the Anti-Homosexual Security Campaign in the Canadian Civil Service." *Le Travail* 35 (1995): 133–161.

——— "Wolfenden in Canada: within and beyond Official Discourse in Law Reform Struggles." In *Human Rights, Sexual Orientation, and Gender Identity in the Commonwealth,* edited by Corinne Lennox and Matthew Waites, 183–206. London: University of London Press, 2013.

Koester, Craig R. *The Word of Life: A Theology of John's Gospel.* Grand Rapids: Eerdmans, 2008.

Lee, Justin. *Torn: Rescuing the Gospel from the Gays vs. Christians Debate.* New York: Jericho, 2012.

Lennox, Corinne, and Matthew Waites, eds. *Human Rights, Sexual Orientation and Gender Identity in the Commonwealth.* London: University of London Press, 2013.

Lewis, C.S. *The Four Loves.* London: Harper Collins, 1960.

Lieu, Judith M. *The Theology of the Johannine Epistles.* Cambridge: Cambridge University Press, 1997.

Life, Patricia. "Outside the Nursing-Home Narrative: Race and Gender Exclusions in Green Grass, Running Water." In *Care Home Stories: Aging, Disability, and Long Term Residential Care,* edited by Sally Chivers and Ulla Kriebernegg, 191–201. Bielefeld: Transcript Verlag, 2017.

Mack, Wayne A. *Strengthening Your Marriage. 2nd edition.* Phillipsburg, NJ: P&R, 1999.

Malina, Bruce J., and Richard L. Rohrbaugh. *Social Science Commentary on the Gospel of John.* Minneapolis: Fortress, 1998.

Maloney, Francis J. *The Gospel of John.* Sacra Pagina Series, edited by Daniel J. Harrington. Collegeville, MN: Liturgical, 1998.

Marin, Andrew. *Love Is an Orientation: Elevating the Conversation with the Gay Community.* Downers Grove: InterVarsity, 2009.

Massey, James Earl. "Reading the Bible as African Americans." In *The New Interpreter's Bible,* edited by Leander E. Keck, vol. 1. 154-160. Nashville: Abingdon, 1995.

McGrath, Alister. *A Passion for Truth: The Intellectual Coherence of Evangelicalism.* Downers Grove: InterVarsity, 1996.

McHugh, Paul. "Transgenderism: A Pathogenic Meme." https://www.thepublic discourse.com/2015/06/15145/

Michaels, J. Ramsey. *The Gospel of John*. New International Commentary on the New Testament, edited by Gordon D. Fee. Grand Rapids: Eerdmans, 2010.

Moltmann, Jürgen. *The Source of Life: The Holy Spirit and the Theology of Life*. Translated by Margaret Kohl. Minneapolis: Fortress, 1997.

Newheiser, David. "Sexuality and Christian Tradition: Innovation and Fidelity, Ancient and Modern." *Journal of Religious Ethics* 43:1 (2015) 122–145.

Nicol, Nancy, et al. *Envisioning Global LGBT Human Rights: (Neo)Colonialism, Neoliberalism, Resistance, and Hope*. London: University of London Press, 2018.

Oden, Thomas C. *After Modernity . . . What? Agenda for Theology*. Grand Rapids: Zondervan, 1992.

Oord, Thomas Jay. *Defining Love: A Philosophical, Scientific, and Theological Engagement*. Grand Rapids: Brazos, 2010.

Ontario Council of Agencies Serving Immigrants. "Glossary of Terms." http://www.positivespaces.ca/sites/positivespaces.ca/files/Glossary%20of%20Terms.pdf.

Ontario Human Rights Commission. "Policy on Preventing Discrimination Because of Gender Identity and Gender Expression." http://www.ohrc.on.ca/en/policy-preventing-discrimination-because-gender-identity-and-gender-expression.

Osiek, Carolyn. "Reading the Bible as Women." In *The New Interpreter's Bible*, edited by Leander E. Keck, 1:181–187. Nashville: Abingdon, 1995.

Paris, Jenell Williams. *The End of Sexual Identity: Why Sex is Too Important to Define Who We Are*. Downers Grove: IVP, 2011.

Perry, Jackie Hill. *Gay Girl, Good God: The Story of Who I Was and Who God Has Always Been*. Nashville: B&H, 2018.

Platt, David. *A Compassionate Call to Counter Culture*. Carol Stream, IL: Tyndale, 2015.

Poirier, Marjorie. "The Concepts of Gender Identity, Gender Expression and Assigned Sex within Drama Therapy: An Interpretative Phenomenological Analysis." Master's Research Paper, Concordia University, 2016.

Reilly, Robert R. *Making Gay Okay: How Rationalizing Homosexual Behaviour is Changing Everything*. San Francisco: Ignatius, 2014.

Rogers, Eugene F., Jr. "Same-Sex Complementarity: A Theology of Marriage." *The Christian Century* 128 (2011): 26–29.

Schlabach, Gerald W. "What Is Marriage Now? A Pauline Case for Same-Sex Marriage." *The Christian Century* 131 (2014): 22–25.

Schleiermacher, F.E.D. *The Christian Faith*. Edinburgh: T&T Clark, 1928.

Schuchard, Bruce G. *1–3 John: A Theological Exposition of Sacred Scripture*. Concordia Commentary, edited by Dean O. Wenthe. Saint Louis, MO: Concordia, 2012.

Scruton, Roger. "Is Sex Necessary? Roger Scruton Analyzes the Poverty of Progressivism's Fixation on Sexual Liberation." *First Things* 248 (2014): 33–37.

Shidlo, Ariel, et al., eds. *Sexual Conversion Therapy: Ethical, Clinical and Research Perspectives.* New York: Haworth Medical, 2001.

Teetzel, Sarah. "Transgender Eligibility Policies in Sport: Science, Ethics, and Evidence." In *Reflecting on Modern Sport in Ancient Olympia: Proceedings of the 2016 Meeting of the International Association for the Philosophy of Sport at the International Olympic Academy,* edited by Heather L. Reid and Eric Moore, 161–70. Fonte Aretusa; Parnassos, 2017.

Teich, Nicholas M. *Transgender 101: A Simple Guide to a Complex Issue.* New York: Colombia University Press, 2012.

Terry, Milton S. *Biblical Hermeneutics.* Grand Rapids: Zondervan, 1974.

Therkelsen, Margaret. *The Love Exchange: An Adventure in Prayer.* Eugene, OR: Wipf and Stock, 1998.

Thurman, Howard. *Jesus and the Disinherited.* Boston: Beacon, 1996.

Townsley, Jeramy. "Queer Sects in Patristic Commentaries on Romans 1:26–27: Goddess Cults, Free Will, and Sex Contrary to Nature?" *Journal of the American Academy of Religion* 81 (2013) 56–79.

Vines, Matthew. *God and the Gay Christian: The Biblical Case in Support of Same Sex Relationships.* New York: Convergent, 2014.

Volf, Miroslav. *Exclusion and Embrace: A Theological Exploration of Identity, Otherness, and Reconciliation.* Nashville: Abingdon, 1996.

Webb, William. *Slaves, Women and Homosexuals: Exploring the Hermeneutics of Cultural Analysis.* Downers Grove: IVP Academic, 2001.

Weiss, Douglas. *Clean: A Proven Plan for Men Committed to Sexual Integrity.* Nashville: Thomas Nelson, 2013.

Whitehead, Andrew L. "Male and Female He Created Them: Gender Traditionalism, Masculine Images of God, and Attitudes Towards Same-Sex Unions." *Journal for the Scientific Study of Religion* 53 (2014) 479–496.

Whitehead, James D. and Evelyn Eaton Whitehead. "Transgender Lives: From Bewilderment to God's Extravagance" *Pastoral Psychology* 63 (2014): 171–184.

Yarhouse, Mark A. *Homosexuality and the Christian.* Bloomington, MN: Bethany House, 2010.

———. *Listening to Sexual Minorities.* Downers Grove: InterVarsity, 2018.

———. *Understanding Gender Dysphoria: Navigating Transgender Issues in a Changing Culture.* Downers Grove: InterVarsity, 2015.

———. *Understanding Sexual Identity: A Resource for Youth Ministry.* Grand Rapids: Zondervan, 2013.

Yarhouse, Mark A., and Julia Sadusky. *Emerging Gender Identities: Understanding the Diverse Experiences of Today's Youth.* Grand Rapids: Brazos, 2020.

Zizioulas, John D. *Being as Communion: Studies in Personhood and the Church.* New York: St Vladimir's Seminary Press, 1985.

Subject Index

Scripture Index